DATE DUE

THE WORLD
OF H. G. WELLS

THE WORLD OF H. G. WELLS

BY

VAN WYCK BROOKS

HASKELL HOUSE PUBLISHERS Ltd.
Publishers of Scarce Scholarly Books
NEW YORK. N. Y. 10012
1969

First Published 1915

HASKELL HOUSE PUBLISHERS LTD.
Publishers of Scarce Scholarly Books
280 LAFAYETTE STREET
NEW YORK, N. Y. 10012

Library of Congress Catalog Card Number: **72-92949**

Standard Book Number 8383-0962-3

Printed in the United States of America

To
Max Lippitt Larkin

CONTENTS

THE WORLD OF H. G. WELLS

INTRODUCTION

A NATURAL pause appears to have come in the career of Mr. H. G. Wells. After so many years of travelling up and down through time and space, familiarizing himself with all the various parts of the solar system and presenting himself imaginatively at all the various geological epochs, from the Stone Age to the end of the world, he has for good and all domesticated himself in his own planet and point of time. This gradual process of slowing down, so to speak, had been evident from the moment of his first appearance. The most obvious fact about his romances of science, considered as a series, is that each one more nearly approached the epoch in which we live, and the realities of this epoch. From the year A. D. 802,701, witnessed in his first romance by the Time Traveller, we found ourselves at last in the presence of a decade only so remote as that

of the war which has now befallen Europe. A
similar tendency in his novels has been equally
marked. The possibilities of science and socialism have received a diminishing attention
relatively beside the possibilities of human re-
action to science and socialism. It is individual men and women, and the motives and
personalities of individual men and women,
which now concern him. Still retaining the entire planet as the playground of his ideas, still
upholding science and socialism as his essential heroes, he has been driven by experience to
approach these things through human nature
as it is. In a recent essay he has told us not
to expect any more dramatic novelties: for the
present at any rate our business must be to
make science and socialism feel at home.
Whether or not this may stand as a general
diagnosis of our epoch, it is a remarkable confession with regard to his own place in it. For
it signifies nothing less than that he has
reached the limit of his own circle of ideas and
finished his own pioneering, and that his work
for the future will be to relate the discoveries
of his youth with human experience. He is no

longer a "new voice"; his work belongs, for good or ill, to history and literature, and he presents himself from this time forward as a humanist.

In this new posture Wells does not stand alone. He is typical of an entire generation of Englishmen that knows not Oxford, a generation which has been busy with all manner of significant movements and discoveries, too busy indeed to relate them to the common reason of humankind. During these years the word "academic" has been outlawed; naturally so, for the academic mind is to the creative mind what the digestive system is to the human body: a period of energetic exercise must precede its operation. But in order that ideas may be incorporated in society they must submit themselves at the right moment to those digestive processes by which they are liquefied and transmitted through the veins to all the various members of the common organism.

During the last twenty years modern thought has been dominated to an extraordinary degree by men who have been educated solely through the movements in which they have taken part: seldom has there been so universal and so hectic an empiricism. But this is the way the earth moves. Like an inchworm it doubles itself up at intervals and then gradually stretches itself straight again. The whole nineteenth century, according to Taine, was occupied in working out two or three ideas concocted in Germany during the Napoleonic era. History is a succession of Gothic invasions and academic subversions. It marks the end of one of those eras which perpetually overlap one another in various groups of men and cycles of thought that our own Visigoths have capitulated. As the pressure of their own immediate points of view relaxes and they cease to identify their own progress with the progress of men in general, they become perhaps less striking but certainly more useful.

Intensely preoccupied with contemporary ideas and inventions, brilliantly gifted and full of life, these leaders of thought were more innocent of literature and history than a freshman. Both Wells and Bernard Shaw have confessed that throughout their most active intellectual careers they believed instinctively that progress was mainly a matter of chronology. To discover the future Wells considered it necessary merely to set his imagination at work on Chicago and multiply it by a thousand; while the famous remark of Shaw that he was "better than Shakespeare" sprang from his assumption that, living three centuries later, he naturally stood (as a dwarf, in his own phrase) upon Shakespeare's shoulders. This naïveté placed them at the mercy of literature, as they soon discovered. Everyone knows the change that came over Bernard Shaw's cosmos when for the first time, a few years ago, he read two or three pre Darwinian philosophers: one could almost have heard a pin drop when he stopped talking about being better than Shakespeare. A similar experience, exhibited in his books, has befallen Wells, and there is no doubt that reading has contributed to the progressive modesty of his point of view. Each monument of historic experience that he has absorbed has left its mark on him. Rabelais, Machiavelli, Plato, incorporated at regular intervals in his own work, have certainly contributed to make him less agile and less dramatic.

Let us take advantage of these post-prandial moments to survey some of the remarkable ideas which have been added to the general stock during this period. After the fashion of Cato, Bernard Shaw and H. G. Wells have come late to the study of Greek. Bernard Shaw read Plato at fifty, and in his latest book Wells has insisted that in the Great State everyone will study Greek. Nothing could signify more plainly that these outriders of the Modern Mind have come to a halt and wish to connect themselves with tradition, with history, with literature, with religion, with the grand current of human experience. Having been for so long experimenting with new and untried forces, sharply separated from what is received and understood, they should be related to the familiar landmarks and connected with the main stream of English thought and literature.

Grotesque and violent as it may at first appear, I believe that in the future Wells will be thought of as having played toward his own

epoch a part very similar to that played by
Matthew Arnold. I say this with full recognition of their remoteness in personal quality,
recognizing also the difference in their direct
objects of attack, in the precise causes they
uphold. One thinks of these two vivid personalities—Wells—how shall one picture him?—
and Matthew Arnold, that superb middle-class
gentleman with his great face and deprecating
hands—and the comparison is instantly ludi-
crous. In reality the entire trend of Arnold's
social criticism was anti-individualistic and in
a straight line with socialism. Seen retrospectively the main work of Wells has not been to
promote any intellectual or economic doctrine,
but to alter the English frame of mind. The
function of each of these men has been to bring
home to the English mind a range of ideas not
traditional in it.

Indeed this comparison holds (the shock
once over) not merely with regard to their
general function, but in their specific attitude
toward most of the branches of thought and
action they have concerned themselves with.
Wells on Education, on Criticism, on Politics

and the nostrums of Liberalism, Wells even on
Religion continues the propaganda of Arnold.
Everywhere in these so superficially dissimilar
writings is exhibited the same fine dissatisfac-
tion, the same faith in ideas and standards, the
same dislike of heated bungling, plunging, wilfulness, and confusion; even the same predom-
inant contempt for most things that are, the
same careful vagueness of ideal. It was Arnold who passed his life in trying to make
England believe in and act upon ideas instead
of "muddling through," who never wearied of
holding up the superiority of everything
French and everything German to everything
English, who adopted into his own language
that phrase about "seeing things as in themselves they really are." Read his chapter on
Our Liberal Practitioners and you will find
the precise attitude of Wells. toward the premature inadequate doing of things rather than
the continued research, experiment, and discipline which lead to right fulfilments. Who
urged the ventilation of life, affairs, conduct
in the light of world experience? Who
preached the gospel of reasonableness, mutual

understanding, and more light? Who spurred England to cultivate the virtue of intellectual curiosity? Who believed with a paradoxical passion in coolness and detachment? In each of these things what Arnold was to his generation Wells remarkably has been to ours. Differing in their view of the substance of religion, their conception of the Church as a great common receptacle for the growing experience of the race is precisely the same, fragmentation, segregation, sectarianism being to both of them in this matter the greatest of evils. The love of curiosity, centrality, ventilation, detachment, common understanding, coolness and reasonableness and a realistic vision, the dislike of confusion, bungling, wilfulness, incompetence, hot-headedness, complacency, sectarianism—these are quite fundamental traits, and Arnold and Wells share them in a remarkable degree. It is quite true that Arnold lived in a universe which only with some reluctance confessed to three dimensions, while that of Wells trembles with the coming of a fourth. But in any case it is worth while to release a phenomenon like Wells from the medium of

purely contemporary influences, and for this
purpose it is convenient to see a socialist in
the light of a man who knew nothing of socialism, to see that socialism is itself a natural
outgrowth of those "best things that have
been thought and said in the world." It
is important to realize that the train of thought
and the circle of ideas of this man are connected with a well-recognized branch of intellectual tradition. And even socialism is bene-
fitted by having friends at court.

CHAPTER I

THE FIRST PHASE

"I AM, by a sort of predestination, a social-ist," Wells wrote once. And everything one can say of him serves merely to explain, justify, qualify, illuminate and refine that statement.

First of all it implies a certain disposition and certain habits of mind, habits of mind which are all to be found in the first phase of his work, in those marvellous tales of Time and Space that won him his original sensational fame. It is this disposition behind them, this quality they have as of an inevitable attitude toward life and the world, which distinguishes them at once from those other superficially similar tales of Jules Verne. The marvels of Jules Verne are just marvels, delightful, irresponsible plunderings from a helpless universe. To the grown-up mind they have a little of that pathetic futility one associates with a millionaire's picture-gallery, where all sorts of things have been brought together, without any exercise of inevitable personal choice, because they are expensive. I don't know that the tales of Wells are better tales, but they have that ulterior synthetic quality that belongs to all real expressions of personality. Wells was never merely inventive; his invention was the first stage of an imaginative growth.

Now the quality that pervades all these early writings is what may be called a sense of the infinite plasticity of things. He conceived a machine that could travel through time, a man who found a way to become invisible, a drug that made men float like balloons, another drug that enabled men to live a thousand hours in one, a crystal egg through which one could watch the life in Mars, a man who could stop the sun like Joshua, a food that turned men into giants, a biologist who discovered a method of carving animals into men, an angel who visited a rural vicar, a mermaid who came to earth in search of a soul, a homicidal orchid, a gigantic bird hatched from a prehistoric egg, a man who passed outside space. In short, the universe appeared to him like that magic shop of which he also wrote, where the most astonishing things may happen, if you are the Right Sort of Boy.

If all this implies anything it implies that things in general are not fixed and static, but that they are, on the contrary, infinitely plastic, malleable, capable of responding to any purpose, any design you may set working among them. The universe, it seems to assume, may be and quite possibly is proceeding after some logical method of its own, but so far as man is concerned this method appears to be one of chance. Obviously, man can do the most surprising things in it, can take as it were all sorts of liberties with it. The universe, in short, is like a vacant field which may or may not belong to some absent landlord who has designs of his own upon it; but until this absent landlord appears and claims his field, all the children in the neighborhood can build huts in it and play games upon it and, in a word, for all practical purposes, consider it their own.

This idea of the relation between free will and determinism is the underlying assumption of Wells, as he explains it in *First and Last Things:*

> Take life at the level of common sensations and common experience and there is no more indisputable fact than man's freedom of will, unless it is his complete moral responsibility. But make only the least penetrating of scientific analyses and you perceive a world of inevitable consequences, a rigid succession of cause and effect.

And elsewhere he says:

> On the scientific plane one is a fatalist. . . . But does the whole universe of fact, the external world about me, the mysterious internal world from which my motives rise, form one rigid and fated system as Determinists teach? I incline to that belief. . . . From me as a person this theory of predestination has no practical value. . . . I hesitate, I choose just as though the thing was unknowable. For me and my conduct there is that much wide practical margin of freedom. I am free and freely and responsibly making the future —so far as I am concerned.

In a word, for all the purposes that affect man's need the universe is infinitely plastic and

amenable to his will. Like every clean-cut
philosophical conception, this clears the ground
for practical conduct and a certain sort of direct action.

There was a time, no doubt, when he shared
the old Utopian folly of expecting a sudden
and unanimous change of human will. When
the universe appears as unconventional as it
used to appear to Wells, there can surely be no
reason to think it impossible, after a comet has
collided with the world, for the human race to
become suddenly Utopian. Generally speaking, comets do not collide with the world, and
in the same way men are slow to change. But
certainly if Wells ever thought of humanity as
merely a multiplication of one pattern, certainly if he has long since abandoned the idea
of our all turning over a new leaf one fine
morning, he has never lost his faith in free will
as regards the individual. He has always believed in the personal doctrine of summarily
"making an end to things" as distinguished
from the old-fashioned doctrine of "making the
best of things"; and there is nothing more mod-

ern about him than his aversion to the good old
English theory of "muddling through."

Mr. Polly is a good example of his view of
personal direct action, the getting rid, quickly
and decisively, of a situation that has only sentiment to save it from complete demoralization.
"When a man has once broken through the
wall of every-day circumstances," he remarks at
the moment of the Polly *débâcle,* "he has made
a discovery. If the world does not please you,
you can change it. Determine to alter it at any
price, and you can change it altogether." Mr.
Polly sets fire to his shop, takes to the road and
repairs his digestion. Desertion of duty and
the quick repudiation of entanglements make
him healthy and sensible and give him a sense
of purpose in things. And I know of nothing
in all Wells that is described with more relish
than that Beltane festival which occurs toward
the end of *In the Days of the Comet.* The
world's great age has begun anew, and the enlightened men of the new time revive the May
Day of old in order to burn the useless trap-
pings of the past. They heap old carpets on
the fire, ill-designed furniture, bad music and

cheap pictures, stuffed birds, obsolete school-books, dog-eared penny fiction, sham shoes, and all the corrugated iron in the world; every tangible thing that is useless, false, disorderly, accidental, obsolete, and tawdry to celebrate the beginning of things that are clean, beautiful, and worthy. Sceptical, hesitant, and personal as Wells has become, that indicates a strong primitive mental trait. Philosophy does not spring out of the brain; we hate the hateful things of our own experience, just as we think the things we desire. And though there are nine and sixty ways of being a socialist, they all unite in a certain sense of the plasticity and malleability of things human, a certain faith in the possibility of asserting order in the midst of disorder and intelligently cleaning house.

Inherent in this trait is another—detachment. You only become aware of confusion when you stand free of it, when you cease to be a part of it. And of all writers who have so immediately felt life I doubt if there has been one so detached as Wells. The mental detachment of his early tales is a detachment half scientific, half artistic; scientific as of one who sees things experimentally in their material, molecular aspect, artistic as of one conscious of moulding will and placed amid plastic material. Thus, for example, he sees human beings quite stripped of their distinctively human qualities; he sees men anatomically, as in that passage where the Invisible Man, killed with a spade, becomes visible again as a corpse:

> Everyone saw, faint and transparent as though it were made of glass, so that veins and arteries and bones and nerves could be distinguished, the outline of a hand, a hand limp and prone. It grew clouded and opaque even as they stared. . . . And so, slowly, beginning at his hands and feet and creeping along his limbs to the vital centres of his body, that strange change continued. First came the little white nerves, a hazy gray stretch of a limb, then the glossy bones and intricate arteries, then the flesh and skin, first a faint fogginess, then growing rapidly dense and opaque.

Similar is a passage in *A Story of the Days to Come,* where he describes an ordinary breakfast of our own day: "the rude masses of bread needing to be carved and smeared over with animal fat before they could be made palatable, the still recognizable fragments of recently killed animals, hideously charred and hacked." That surely is quite as a man from another planet, or a chemist after a long day's work in the laboratory, would view our familiar human things. And one recalls another sentence from *Kipps* where this detachment links itself with a deeper social insight and hints at the part it had come to play in Wells's later mind: "I see through the darkness," he says, toward the end of the book, "the souls of my Kippses as they are, *as little pink strips of quivering, living stuff,* as things like the bodies of little ill-nourished, ailing, ignorant children—children who feel pain, who are naughty and muddled and suffer, and do not understand why."

And just as he sees men and human things chemically and anatomically, so he sees the world astronomically. He has that double quality (like his own Mr. Bessel) of being bodily very active in life and at the same time watching it from a great distance. In his latest book he has figured a god looking on from the clouds; and there is nothing in his novels more stimulating and more uncanny than a certain faculty of telescoping his view sud-

denly from the very little to the very large,
expanding and contracting his vision of things
at will. You find the germ of this faculty
in his early tales. Looking down as though
from a balloon he sees the world as a planet,
as a relatively small planet. In doing so he
maintains at first a purely scientific set of
values; he is not led, as he has since been led,
and as Leopardi was led by the same imaginative experience, to adopt poetical values
and to feel acutely the littleness and the pow-
erlessness of man. His values remain scientific, and the absurdity he feels is the absurdity
an astronomer must feel, that in so small
a space men can vaunt themselves and squab-
ble with one another. Race prejudice, for
example, necessarily appears to him as foolish as it would appear to ordinary eyes
among insects that happen to be swarming on
a fallen apple. Once you get it into your mind
that the world is a ball in space, you find a peculiar silliness in misunderstandings on that
ball. This reflection has led to many views of
life; in Wells it led to a sense of the need of
human solidarity.

And solidarity implies order. The sense of order is one of those instincts exhibited everywhere in the writings of Wells that serve as preliminaries to his social philosophy. There is a passage in *Kipps* where he pictures the satisfactions of shopkeeping to an elect soul: "There is, of course, nothing on earth," he says, "and I doubt at times if there is a joy in heaven, like starting a small haberdasher's shop. Imagine, for example, having a drawerful of tapes, or again, an array of neat, large packages, each displaying one sample of hooks and eyes. Think of your cottons, your drawer of colored silks," etc. De Foe knew a similar satisfaction and has pictured it in *Robinson Crusoe*. De Foe was himself a shopkeeper, just as Wells has been in one of his incarnations; and he knew that good shopkeeping is the microcosm of all good political economy. The satisfaction of a thoroughly competent man who is thrown on a desert island, and sets to work to establish upon it a political economy for one, is a satisfaction by itself. That certainly is a primitive relish, and it is one of the first gestures of Wells's sociology.

Now the sense of solidarity, the sense of order, implies the subordination of details, the discipline of constituent units. Only in his later works did Wells begin to consider the problems of the individual life; in his novels he has considered them almost exclusively, but always in relation to the constructive purpose of society and as what may be called human reservations from it. The telescope has been adjusted to a close range, and the wider relationships are neither so emphasized nor so easily discerned. Nevertheless it is still the world that matters to Wells—the world, the race, the future; not the individual human being. And if, relatively, he has become more interested in the individual and less in the world, that is because he is convinced that the problems of the world can best be approached through the study of individuals. His philosophy has grown less abstract in harmony with his own experience; but the first sketch of his view of human nature and its function is to be found crudely outlined in the scientific romances. How does it figure there?

The human beings who flit through these

early tales are all inconspicuous little men,
whose private existence is of no account, and
who exist to discover, invent, perform all sorts
of wonderful experiments which almost invariably result in their summary and quite unim-
portant destruction. They are merely, in the
most complete sense, experiments in the collective purpose, and their creator has toward
them just the attitude of an anatomist toward
the animals upon which he is experimenting;
not indifferent to their suffering as suffering,
but ignoring it in the spirit of scientific detachment necessary to subordinate means to an end.
"I wanted—it was the only thing I wanted—to
find out the limit of plasticity in a living form,"
says Dr. Moreau in his confession; "and the
study has made me as remorseless as nature."

Invariably these experiments in human possibility, placed in a world where charity is not
so strong as fear, die quite horribly. Dr.
Moreau is destroyed by the beasts he is at-
tempting to vivisect into the semblance of men,
the Invisible Man is battered to death with a
spade, the Visiting Angel burns to death in at-
tempting to carry out his celestial errand, the

man who travels to the moon cannot get back
alive. Does not all this foreshadow the burden
of the later novels, that the individual who
plans and wills for the race is destroyed and
broken by the jealousy, prejudice and inertia in
men and the blind immemorial forces of nature
surging through himself? These are the forces
that are figured, in the early tales, by that horrible hostile universe of nature, and the little in-
trepid men moving about in the midst of it.
And the mind of Wells is always prepared for
the consequences of what it engenders. The
inevitable result of creating an imaginary
world of malignant vegetables and worse than
antediluvian monsters is that the imaginary
men you also create shall suffer through them.
You reverse the order of evolution and return
men to conditions where life is cheap. An
imagination which has accustomed itself to running loose among planets and falling stars,
which has lived habitually in a universe where
worlds battle with one another, is prepared to
stomach a little needless bloodshed. The in-
flexible pursuit of an end implies the sacrifice
of means, and if your experiment happens to

be an invisible man you will produce the invisibility even though it kills the man.

Widen the range and this proposition logically transmutes itself into a second: if your experiment happens to be an orderly society you will produce order at the expense of everything that represents disorder. And from the point of view of a collective purpose, ends, motives and affections that are private and have no collective significance represent disorder. Now the whole purpose of Wells's later work has been to illuminate and refine this proposition. He has flatly distinguished between two sorts of human nature, the constructive, experimental sort which lives essentially for the race, and the acquiescent, ineffectual sort which lives essentially for itself or the established fact; and he gives to his experimental men and women an almost unlimited charter to make ducks and drakes of the ineffectual. Think of the long list of dead and wounded in his novels— Mr. Pope, Mr. Stanley, Mr. Magnet, Mr. Manning, Margaret, Marion—and you realize how much of a certain cruelty, a certain ruthlessness is in the very nature of his philosophy of experimental direct action.

Another primitive relish exhibited in these early tales is the delight of constructing things. The Time Machine, for example, is the work of a mind that immoderately enjoys inventing, erecting, and putting things together; and there is not much difference between constructing an imaginary machine and constructing an imaginary society. If Wells's early Utopian speculations are ingenious impossibilities, are they any more or less so than his mechanical speculations? One doesn't begin life with an overwhelming recognition of the obstacles one may encounter—one doesn't fret too much about the possible, the feasible, or even the logical. It was enough for Wells that he had built his Time Machine, though the logic by which the Time Traveller explains his process is a logic that gives me, at least, a sense of helpless, blinking discomfort—partly, I confess, because to this day I don't believe there is anything the matter with it. In any case it is the sheer delight of construction that fascinates **him, and** everything that is associated with construction fascinates him. He is in love with steel; he speaks with a kind of ecstasy somewhere of "light and clean and shimmering shapes of silvered steel"; steel and iron have for him the transcendental charm that harebells and primroses had for Wordsworth. A world like that in *The Sleeper Awakes*—a world of gigantic machines, air fleets, and the "swimming shadows and enormous shapes" of an engineer's nightmare— is only by afterthought, one feels, the speculation of a sociologist. It expresses the primitive relish of a constructive instinct. It expresses also a sheer curiosity about the future.

In a chapter of his book on America Wells has traced the development of what he calls his prophetic habit of mind as a passage through four stages: the millennial stage of an evangelical childhood when an imminent Battle of Armageddon was a natural thing to be looked for; the stage of ultimate biological possibilities; the stage of prediction by the rule-of-three; and a final stage of cautious anticipation based upon the study of existing facts—a gradual passage from the region of religious or scientific possibilities to the region of human probabilities. "There is no Being but Becoming" was the first of his mental discoveries; and finding years later that Heraclitus had said the same thing, he came to regard the pre-Aristotelian metaphysics as the right point of departure for modern thought. Consider this passage:

I am curiously not interested in things and curiously interested in the consequences of things. . . . I have come to be, I am afraid, even a little insensitive to fine immediate things through this anticipatory habit. . . . This habit of mind confronts and perplexes my sense of things that simply *are,* with my brooding preoccupation with how they will shape presently, what they will lead to, what seed they will sow and how they will wear. At times, I can assure the reader, this quality approaches other-worldliness in its constant reference to an all-important hereafter. There are times indeed when it makes life seem so transparent and flimsy, seem so dissolving, so passing on to an equally transitory series of consequences, that the enhanced sense of instability becomes restlessness and distress; but on the other hand nothing that exists, nothing whatever, remains altogether vulgar or dull and dead or hopeless in its light. . . . But the interest is shifted. The pomp and splendor of established order, the braying triumphs, ceremonies, consummations,— one sees these glittering shows for what they are—through

their threadbare grandeur shine the little significant
things that will make the future.

And the burden of his lecture *The Discovery
of the Future* is that an inductive knowledge of
the future is not only very largely possible, but
is considerably more important for us than the
study of the past.   Even in the sciences, he
says, the test of their validity is their power to
produce confident forecasts.   Astronomy is
based on the forecast of stellar movements,
medical science exists largely for diagnosis.   It
is this thought which determines the nature of
his own sociology.

There is usually something inept in speaking
of a man, and especially an artist, as inter-
changeable with any ism.   Socialism, in the
common sense of the word, is a classification of
men.   Individual socialists are as a rule something more than socialists; often they are socialists by necessity, or imagination, or sentiment, or expediency—their socialism is not inherent, not the frame of their whole being.   In
the degree that socialism is a classification, or a
school of thought, or an economic theory, the
individual socialist will, in practice, make men-

tal reservations from it. Now my whole aim
in this chapter has been to suggest that if socialism had not existed Wells would have invented it. It is not something which at a given
moment or even after a long process of imaginative conversion or conviction came into his
life. It is, in his own formulation of it, the
projection of his whole nature, the expression
of his will, the very content of his art. With
one or two exceptions—works deliberately devoted to propaganda or exposition—even his
purely sociological writings are subjective
writings, personal and artistic in motive; socialism figures in them just as Catholicism figures in the masses of Mozart, or the brother-
hood of man in the poems of Whitman, not as
a cause but as a satisfying conception of truth.
And just as, if one were to study the psychology of Mozart or Whitman, one would find
habits of mind that inevitably produced the individual Catholicism of the one and the individual fraternalism of the other; so behind the
socialism of Wells are certain habits of mind,
certain primitive likes, relishes, instincts, preferences: a faith in free will, a sense of order and

the subordination of details to design, a personal detachment, a pleasure in construction, a curiosity about the future.

These are innate qualities, which inevitably produced their own animating purpose.

CHAPTER II

TOWARDS SOCIALISM

OF all the battered, blurred, ambiguous coins of speech there is none so battered, blurred, and ambiguous as the word socialism. It mothers a dozen creeds at war with one another. And the common enemy looks on, fortified with the Socratic irony of the "plain man," who believes he has at last a full excuse for not understanding these devious doings.

Therefore I take refuge in saying that H. G. Wells is an artist, neither more nor less, that socialism is to him at bottom an artistic idea, and that if it had not existed in the world he would have invented it. This clears me at once of the accusing frowns of any possible Marxian reader, and it also states a truth at the outset. For if the orthodox maintain that socialism is not an affair of choices, may I not retort that here actually is a mind that chooses to make it so? Here is an extraordinary kind of

40

Utopian who has all the equipment of the orthodox and yet remains detached from orthodoxy. Orthodoxy is always jealous of its tabernacles and will not see itself dramatically; it has no concern with artistic presentations. But I protest there ought to be no quarrel here. If a socialism fundamentally artistic is an offence to the orthodox, let them accept it, without resentment, as a little harmless fun— all art being that.

Having said so much I return to my own difficulty, for it is very hard to focus H. G. Wells. He has passed through many stages and has not yet attained the Olympian repose. Artist as he is, he has been hotly entangled in practical affairs. There are signs in his early books that he once shared what Richard Jeffries called the "dynamite disposition,"—even now he knows, in imagination alone, the joy of black destruction. He has also been, and ceased to be, a Fabian. But it is plain that he has passed for good and all beyond the emotional plane of propaganda. He has abandoned working-theories and the deceptions of the intellect which make the man of action. He has become at once more practical and more mystical than a party programme permits one to be. Here is a world where things are being done—a world of which capital and labor are but one interpretation. How far can these things and the men who do them be swept into the service of the race? That is the practical issue in his mind, and the mystical issue lies in the intensity and quality of the way in which he feels it.

To see him clearly one has to remember that he is not a synthetic thinker but a sceptical artist, whose writings are subjective even when they seem to be the opposite, whose personality is constantly growing, expanding, changing, correcting itself ("one can lie awake at night and hear him grow," as Chesterton says), and who believes moreover that truth is not an absolute thing but a consensus of conflicting individual experiences, a "common reason" to be wrought out by constant free discussion and the comparison and interchange of personal discoveries and ideas. He is not a sociologist, but, so to say, an artist of society; one of those thinkers who are disturbed by

the absence of right composition in human
things, by incompetent draughtsmanship and
the misuse of colors, who see the various
races of men as pigments capable of har-
monious blending and the planet itself as a
potential work of art which has been daubed
and distorted by ill-trained apprentices.   In
Wells this planetary imagination forms a permanent and consistent mood, but it has the consistency of a mood and not the consistency of a
system of ideas.   And though he springs from
socialism and leads to socialism, he can only
be called a socialist in the fashion—to adopt a
violently disparate comparison—that St. Fran-
cis can be called a Christian.   That is to say,
no vivid, fluctuating human being, no man of
genius can ever be embodied in an institution.
He thinks and feels it afresh; his luminous,
contradictory, shifting, evanescent impulses
may, on the whole, ally him with this or that
aggregate social view, but they will not let him
be subdued to it.   As a living, expanding organism he will constantly urge the fixed idea
to the limit of fluidity.   So it is with Wells.
There are times when he seems as whimsical

as the wind and as impossible to photograph as a chameleon.

Just here I should like to give what may be taken as his own view of capital and labor socialism in relation to the constructive socialism he himself has at heart. I am putting together certain brief passages from *The Passionate Friends*:

I have come to believe now that labor problems are problems only by the way. They have played their part in a greater scheme. . . . With my innate passionate desire to find the whole world purposeful, I cannot but believe that. . . . Strangest of saviours, there rises over the conflicts of men the glittering angular promise of the machine. There is no longer any need for slavery, open or disguised. We do not need slaves nor toilers nor mere laborers any more; they are no longer essential to a civilization. Man has ridden on his brother man out of the need of servitude. He struggles through to a new phase, a phase of release, a phase when leisure and an unexampled freedom are possible to every human being. . . .

Human thought has begun to free itself from individual entanglements and dramatic necessities and accidental standards. It becomes a collective mind, a collective will towards achievement, greater than individuals or cities or kingdoms or peoples, a mind and will to which we all contribute and which none of us may command nor compromise by our private errors. It ceases to be aristocratic; it detaches itself from persons and takes possession of us all. We are involved as it grows free and dominant, we find ourselves in spite of ourselves, in spite of quarrels and jealousies and conflicts, helping and serving in the making of a new world-city, a new greater State above our legal States, in which all human life becomes a splendid enterprise, free and beautiful. . . .

I have long since ceased to trouble about the economics of human society. Ours are not economic but psychological difficulties. . . .

These last two sentences really tell the whole story. To pass from economics to psychology is to pass from Man to men, from society as a direct object of attack to the individuals who compose it. And this marks the evolution of Wells the romancer and Wells the expositor of socialist doctrine into Wells the novelist. It is the problems of human interaction that occupy him now. But informing these problems, reaching behind and embracing them, is a general view of the world which has only become more intimate, more personal, and more concrete with time.

When, in *New Worlds for Old*, Wells set himself to explain socialism as he conceived it, he assumed as his first principle a certain Good Will in men, an operating will steadily working in life toward betterment. In other words, he supplemented the ordinary socialist idea of economic determinism, which may or may not inevitably bring about order on the industrial plane, with a constructive purpose, which, in his view, can alone bring about the salvation of the race. But this Good Will is not a fatality; it exists only by virtue of remaining a conscious effort. In his experiments in Time and Space Wells had accustomed himself to seeing that the immense possibilities of what might be, so far as the universe is concerned, predetermined things, were, so far as man is concerned, matters of chance. To human society at least, if not to our planet, the most unpropitious things are possible in the future; and there is no reason to suppose that the destiny of the universe, which at every turn cuts athwart the destiny of every species contained in it, should, left to itself, work favorably to man.

This notion is in itself quite outside socialism and does not necessarily lead into socialism. It

was Huxley who said that the world and the
universe, society and nature, are demonstrably
at cross purposes, and that man has to pit his
microcosm against the macrocosm.   Huxley,
in his famous lecture on *Ethics and Evolution,*
went on from this to a kind of informal and
unavowed socialism, figuring society as a well-
tended garden preserved by man's careful art
from the ravages and invasions of that hostile
world of chance, with its gigantic weeds and
blind impulsions, which everywhere lies wait-
ing round about it.   Our work, he implied,
must be in every way to minimize for ourselves the elements of chance, to become aware
of our species in a collective sense, battling with
nature and moulding our own future.

I do not suppose that Wells consciously
adopted this idea from Huxley.   In itself that
would be of little consequence, except so far
as it shows the continuity of thought and the
development of socialism out of science.   But
Wells was for several years a pupil of Huxley, and it is reasonably plain that the mood
in which he wrote his scientific romances was
strongly impregnated by Huxley's influence.

The sinister, incalculable, capricious, destructive forces outside man are symbolized, as I have said, by those colliding comets, invading Martians, and monstrous creatures among which the earlier Wells moved and had his being; just as the sinister, incalculable, capricious forces within man which urge him to destruction form so great a part of his later novels. Most of his heroes (typified in *The New Machiavelli*) come to grief through the blind irrational impulsions within themselves. And he is equally haunted by what he has called the "Possible Collapse of Civilization." I do not know how much this is due to an evangelical childhood, in which Time, Death, and Judgment are always imminent; how much to an overbalancing study of science at the expense of the humanities; how much to an overdeveloped sense of the hazard that life is; and how much to plain facts. But there it is: it has always been a fixed conviction with Wells that man personal and man social is dancing on a volcano.

Therefore he has come to socialism not by the ordinary course but by a route obscure and

lonely. The sense of possible catastrophe and
collapse, the folly of leaving things to chance,
the infinite waste and peril of committing our
affairs to nature rather than to art—these are
some of the negative reasons that have made
it impossible for him to fall in with the non-
socialist ideal in human affairs, that "broaden-
ing down from precedent to precedent" which
he calls "muddling through": a doctrine that is
wholly compatible with a world of haphazard
motives, accidental fortunes, accidental management, a democratic individualism that
places power in irresponsible hands and sup-
presses talents that society cannot afford to
lose, a governmental system that concerns itself with legal and financial arrangements,
experts with no sense of a common purpose,
patriotisms that thrive on international bad
feelings, and that competitive principle which
succeeds in the degree in which it ignores the
general welfare—a chaos of private aims,
private virtues, private motives, without any
collective human design at all.

In the light of these opposed ideas of society
as a thing of Chance and as a thing of Design,

let me run over two or three of the tales of Wells.

First of all there is the special *laissez faire* of pure economic determinism. *The Time Machine* pictures a possible result of the Marxian process which has led to an irrevocable division of classes. The rich, who were, in the old time, in comparison with the poor, disciplined and united, have long since reached a point where work and fear are for them things of the past. They occupy the surface of the earth, and idleness and futility have made them light-headed, puny, helpless creatures, stirring about and amusing themselves in the sunlight. The poor, meanwhile, driven underground where they burrow and tend machinery and provide, have lost all human semblance and become white, horrible ghoul-like creatures that see in the dark; at night they swarm out of their holes and feed upon the creatures of the upper air. The one class has lost all power to defend itself and the other all pity to spare, and gradually, year after year, mankind comes to its end.

Then there is the ordinary *laissez faire* of

capitalism, a result of which is pictured in *The Sleeper Awakes.* The Sleeper, one recalls, awakens four generations hence to find himself the master-capitalist, owner of half the world, and the world is one where capital and labor have irrevocably destroyed the possibility of a constructive human scheme. But the responsibility for that future is very ingeniously placed upon us of the present time; for Graham's ownership of the world is the outcome of one of those irresponsible whims that in our day characterize the whole individualistic view of property. His cousin, having no family to inherit his possessions, has left the whole in trust for the Sleeper, half in jest, expecting him never to waken; and in time the trustees of this vested fund have become the irresponsible bureaucrats of the world. "We were making the future," says the awakened Sleeper, looking out upon this monstrous outcome of whim and *laissez faire,* "and hardly any of us troubled to think what future we were making."

Consider also *The Empire of the Ants,* in which Wells has figured a possible reconquest of man by nature, owing to the greater collective discipline of at least one non-human species. He imagines a species of poisonous ants with only a little greater faculty of organized co-operative intelligence than ordinary ants, which have terrorized and finally routed several villages of unintelligent and unorganized Brazilian natives far up the Amazon. The Brazilian government sends against them an outworn inefficient gunboat, with an incompetent captain and a muddle-headed crew; and when they arrive the ants fall upon the only man sent ashore and sting him to death. The captain repeats over and over, "But what can we *do?*" And at last with tremendous decision he fires a gun at them and retires. The story ends with a report that the ants are swarming all over the interior of Brazil and that nobody knows how to prevent them from occupying the whole of South America.

And then there is *The History of Mr. Polly*. I ignore for the moment the individual aspect of his case, for Mr. Polly is not merely an individual—he is an emblem of the whole, he is society *in concreto*. We find him at the opening of the book sitting on a stile, suffering from indigestion and consequently depressed in spirits. It is two o'clock of a Sunday afternoon, and he has just finished his mid-day meal. He has eaten cold potatoes, cold pork, Rashdall's mixed pickles—three gherkins, two onions, a small cauliflower head and several capers; cold suet pudding, treacle and pale cheese, three slices of grey bread, and a jug of beer. He hates himself, he hates his wife, he hates existence. But Mr. Polly's interior, the things that have gone into it and the emotions that rise out of it, are only typical of an entire life that has, to quote Macaulay's eulogy of the British constitution, thought nothing of symmetry and much of convenience.

Each of the novels of Wells, in one aspect at least, presents the accidental nature of our world in some one typical case. *Love and Mr. Lewisham* shows how in the case of one of those young students who have, as things are, no chance at all, but who are the natural builders of a better world, the constructive possibility is crushed by the primary will to live. At

eighteen Mr. Lewisham is an assistant master
at one of those incompetent private-enterprise
schools which for Wells (as also for Matthew
Arnold) epitomize our haphazard civilization.
He has a "future"—the Schema which he pins
to his bedroom wall promises unimaginable
achievements. He marries, and you feel that
he should marry and that he has married the
right person. But then with interests divided
he has to find money and in doing so he fails
in his examinations. At last it becomes a
choice between his career and his children, between the present and the future, and the children and the future win. Society loses just in
the degree that Lewisham himself loses, for he
was fitted to be a builder; and society has first,
in the face of all his efforts, imperfectly
equipped him and then consistently refused to
take advantage of his talents.

Just as Lewisham is a potential builder
of society who is defeated, so Kipps is a specimen of the raw material, the muddled inferior
material with which society has to deal and re-
fuses to deal. Kipps, like Mr. Polly, is from
the beginning a victim of accident, spawned on

the world, miseducated, apprenticed at four-
teen to a Drapery Bazaar. He grows up ignorant, confused, irresponsible; and then suddenly, as accidentally as he was born, has
£26,000 and responsibility thrust upon him.
The fortune of Kipps lifts him at once out of
the obscure negligible world of the populace
and makes him a figure to be reckoned with.
Therein lies the comedy of the book. He
tries to make himself what in his own view a
man of means ought to be; naturally he sees
money not as a force but as a thing to be
spent, and he finds that even from this point of
view he has no freedom of will, and that his
lack of training inevitably places him in the
hands of equally irresponsible persons who
want his money. He wishes to build a house,
designed after his own vaguely apprehended
needs and desires, and somehow under the
wand of the architect a house with eleven bed-
rooms springs from the ground, a house plainly far beyond his own or Ann's power of
management, and the prospect of disrespect-
ful servants, terrifying callers, and a horde of
scheming lawyers, tradesfolk and satellites.

And the life of Kipps under prosperity is summed up in the following dialogue:

> "Wonder what I shall do this afternoon," said Kipps, with his hands deep in his pockets.
> He pondered and lit a cigarette.
> "Go for a walk, I s'pose," said Ann.
> "I *been* for a walk this morning."
> "S'pose I must go for another," he added after an interval.

May one suggest how the significance of such a story as this varies according to the point of view? In the ordinary literature of comedy, Kipps would be merely a parvenu whose want of dignity and ignorance of the right use of money are laughable—or, if the novelist were a humanitarian, pitiful. To the socialist, on the other hand, every incident of his life, every gesture of his mind, is a unique indictment of things as they are. He stands for the whole waste of human stuff in a world which has not learned how to economize itself, whose every detail is accidental in a general chaotic absence of social design.

In this aspect *Tono-Bungay* is the most powerful work of Wells. Just as his romances

of the future had exhibited the possible effects
of accidental heedless social conduct in the
past, so his novels exhibit the motives that produce this heedlessness to consequences. Thus
the world in which the Sleeper awakes, a world
irrevocably ruled by the bureaucratic trustees
of an irresponsible private fortune, is just a
conceivable consequence of such a career as
Uncle Ponderevo's, had not catastrophe over-
whelmed him and enabled Wells to point a
much more pregnant moral. *Tono-Bungay* is
a great epic of irresponsible capitalism from
the socialist point of view. Uncle Ponderevo
is a born commercial meteor, and when he first
enters the book, a small druggist in a dead
country town, he exhibits the temperament of
a Napoleon of finance spoiling for conquest.
He wants to Wake Up Wimblehurst, invent
something, do something, shove something.

He indicated London as remotely over the top of the
dispensing counter, and then as a scene of great activity
by a whirl of the hand and a wink and a meaning smile
at me.
   "What sort of things do they do?" I asked.
   "Rush about," he said. "Do things! Somethin'

glorious. There's cover gambling. Ever heard of that, George?" He drew the air in through his teeth. "You put down a hundred, say, and buy ten thousand pounds' worth. See? That's a cover of one per cent. Things go up one, you sell, realize cent per cent; down, whiff, it's gone! Try again! Cent per cent, George, every day. Men are made or done for in an hour. And the shoutin'! . . . Well, that's one way, George. Then another way—there's Corners!"

"They're rather big things, aren't they?" I ventured.

"Oh, if you go in for wheat and steel—yes. But suppose you tackled a little thing, George. Just some leetle thing that only needed a few thousands. Drugs, for example. Shoved all you had into it—staked your liver on it, so to speak. Take a drug—take ipecac, for example. Take a lot of ipecac. Take all there is! See? There you are! There aren't unlimited supplies of ipecacuanha—can't be!—and it's a thing people *must* have. Then quinine again! You watch your chance, wait for a tropical war breaking out, let's say, and collar all the quinine. Where *are* they? Must have quinine, you know—Eh? . . .

"Lord! there's no end of things—no end of *little* things. Dill-water—all the suff'ring babes yowling for it. Eucalyptus again—cascara—witch hazel—menthol —all the toothache things. Then there's antiseptics, and curare, cocaine. . . .

"Rather a nuisance to the doctors," I reflected.

"They got to look out for themselves. By Jove, yes. They'll do you if they can, and you do them. Like brigands. That makes it romantic. That's the Romance of Commerce, George."

He passed into a rapt dream, from which escaped such fragments as: "Fifty per cent. advance, sir; security—to-morrow."

The idea of cornering a drug struck upon my mind then as a sort of irresponsible monkey trick that no one would ever be permitted to do in reality. It was the sort of nonsense one would talk to make Ewart laugh and set him going on to still odder possibilities. I thought it was part of my uncle's way of talking. But I've learnt differently since. The whole trend of modern money-making is to foresee something that will probably be needed and put it out of reach, and then to haggle yourself wealthy. You buy up land upon which people will presently want to build houses, you secure rights that will bar vitally important developments, and so on, and so on. Of course the naïve intelligence of a boy does not grasp the subtler developments of human inadequacy. He begins life with the disposition to believe in the wisdom of grown-up people, he does not realize how casual and disingenuous has been the development of law and custom, and he thinks that somewhere in the state there is a power as irresistible as a head master's to check mischievous, foolish enterprises of every sort. I will confess that when my uncle talked of cornering quinine, I had a clear impression that any one who contrived to do that would pretty certainly go to gaol. Now I know that any one who could really bring it off would be much more likely to go to the House of Lords!

And such or nearly such is this career. Tono-Bungay, that swindling patent medicine without value or meaning, is the insubstantial hippogriff upon which Uncle Ponderevo soars upward on the wind of advertisement. In a society whose basis is unlimited individual rights, he is able to disorganize the industrial world and to work out his absurd, inept, extravagant destiny, scattering ruin right and left.

But the spirit of Good Will, the disinterested constructive spirit of socialism which is the underlying assumption of Wells, appears here as in all his later books. Out of the wreckage the constructive purpose emerges, in the person of George Ponderevo. It shapes itself as a steel destroyer, the work of an engineer's brain, a destroyer which England has refused and which plunges down the Thames to the open sea, the symbol of man's intentions, without illusions and without the hope of personal gain, the disinterested spirit of science and truth.

CHAPTER III

SOCIALISM "TRUE AND FALSE"

IN the development of intellectual modesty lies the growth of statesmanship. It has been the chronic mistake of statecraft and all organizing spirits to attempt immediately to scheme and arrange and achieve. Priests, schools of thought, political schemers, leaders of men, have always slipped into the error of assuming that they can think out the whole—or, at any rate, completely think out definite parts—of the purpose and future of man, clearly and finally; they have set themselves to legislate and construct on that assumption, and, experiencing the perplexing obduracy and evasions of reality, they have taken to dogma, persecution, training, pruning, secretive education, and all the stupidities of self-sufficient energy.

The man who wrote that is not what is called a whole-hearted man as regards any form of group-action. He does not "fit in." He is at bottom a sceptic, and a sceptic is one who reduces every question to the question of human nature. So that the socialism of Wells is nec-

essarily at variance with all the recognized
group-forms of socialism, Administrative,
Philanthropic, and Revolutionary. I must
briefly indicate in each case what is the quality
of this divergence.

As regards the first, he has a complete dis-
trust of what Hilaire Belloc has called the
"Servile State;" and what he distrusts he viru-
lently dislikes. In his view, Administrative
socialism, as it appears in Sidney Webb and
the Fabian Society, and in the tendency of
contemporary Liberalism, has led to an exces-
sive conservatism toward the existing machinery of government, it has depended altogether
too much on organization without popular
support, and as a result has tended to throw
the whole force of the socialist movement into
a bureaucratic regime of small-minded experts.
The activity of the Fabians especially, he says,
has set great numbers of socialists working in
the old governmental machinery without real-
izing that the machinery should have been re-
constructed first. The whole tendency of this
method, as it is exhibited in the works of the
English Liberal Party of to-day, is toward

a socialization of the poor without a corresponding socialization of the rich; toward a more and more marked chasm between the regimented workers and the free employers.

And it throws the control of affairs into the hands of a mass of highly specialized officials, technical minds, mutually-unenlightened experts. In an age when the progress of society depends upon breaking down professional barriers, when the genuine scientist, for instance, is a man who passes beyond his own science and sees the inter-relationships of all knowledge, the mind which has been trained in one habitual routine is the most dangerous type of mind to place in authority. On the one hand, society depends upon the coöperation of all sorts of specialists, their free discussion, and comparison of methods, results, and aims; on the other experts in office are apt to grow narrow, impatient, and contemptuous, seeing nothing beyond their immediate work,—and this particularly when they have been trained for administration without any wide experience of the world.

Therefore upon experts as such, in distinction from constructive and coöperating specialists, Wells, with all the force of his belief in the ventilating of knowledge and the humanizing of affairs, wages an unceasing war. *The First Men in the Moon* satirizes, after the fashion of Swift, a world where the expert view of life, not only in administration but in all work, prevails. Each inhabitant of the Moon has a single rigidly defined function, to which everything else in his nature is accommodated. Thus certain types of machine-menders are compressed in jars, while others are dwarfed to fit them for fine work, "a really more humane proceeding," as Mr. Cavor observes, "than our method of leaving children to grow into human beings and then making machines of them." And in *The Great State* he returns to his attack on government by experts: "Whatever else may be worked out in the subtler answers our later time prepares, nothing can be clearer than that the necessary machinery of government must be elaborately organized to prevent the development of a managing caste in permanent conspiracy, tacit or expressed, against the normal man." And he adds: "The Great State will, I feel convinced, regard changes in occupation as a proper circumstance in the life of every citizen; it will value a certain amateurishness in its service, and prefer it to the trite omniscience of the stale official." One of the many and increasing indications, one might suggest, of the remarkable tendency in Wells to find good in the old humanistic Tory, as distinguished from the modern bureaucratic Liberal, view of life.

But lest I be tempted to carry this latter suggestion too far just at this point, I pass on to his equally virulent dislike of Philanthropic socialism and the busy Superior Person in affairs; especially the type of political woman so dear to Mrs. Humphry Ward's heart. If the expert bureaucratic point of view represents the action of socialist thought on the Liberal Progressive mind, so also the philanthropic superior point of view represents the action of socialist thought on the Conservative mind. It is arrogant, aggressive, and condescending. It implies the raising of one's inferiors, and what weak mortal should assume that she (for this happens to be a mainly feminine affliction) is the standard according to which other mortals ought to be raised?

Two of these energetic ladies have been pictured with a bitter vividness by Wells in Altiora Bailey and Aunt Plessington, the former summing up the Fabian-expert view, the latter summing up the Superior-philanthropic view. Altiora has "P. B. P."—*pro bono publico*—engraved inside her wedding ring. All the misery of the world she marshals invincibly in statistics. She sees everything as existing in types and classes; she pushes her cause with a hard, scheming, and wholly self-centred eagerness, managing political dinners, indefatigably compiling blue-books, dreaming of a world nailed as tightly and firmly under the rule of experts as a carpet is nailed with brass tacks.

On the other hand Aunt Plessington is the incarnation of a "Movement" somewhat vague in purpose but always aggressively beneficial to the helpless ones of the earth. "Her voice was the true governing-class voice, a strangulated contralto, abundant and authoritative; it made everything she said clear and important,

so that if she said it was a fine morning it was
like leaded print in the *Times*." Her mission
is principally to interfere with the habits and
tastes of the working-class, making it impossible for them to buy tobacco and beer or "the
less hygienic and more palatable forms of
bread (which do not sufficiently stimulate the
coatings of the stomach)." She is, in short,
one of those odious managing people who
know nothing of and care nothing for human
nature, who concern themselves wholly with
the effects without penetrating to the causes
of misery, who see mankind as irrevocably divided into a governing and a governed class,
and whose idea of government is to make the
governed as uncomfortably efficient as possible
and as lacking in free will. She is exactly one
of those arrogant sterile souls, in love with
methods rather than men, who have made the
Servile State an imminent and horrid possibility and have turned so many misinformed
human beings (including Tolstoy) against socialism altogether.

If Wells dislikes Administrative and Philanthropic socialism because they are not suffi-

ciently human, he has an equal aversion to what is called orthodox, that is to say, Revolutionary socialism; and in this he includes all socialism that is fundamentally economic. "I have long since ceased to trouble about the economics of human society," says Stratton in *The Passionate Friends,* in words we are justified in taking as the opinion of Wells himself. "Ours are not economic but psychological difficulties."

That statement is full of meaning. It expresses, not a fact but a personal conviction— the personal conviction with which the psychological constructive socialism of Wells begins. But before I pass on to this I must make one comment that persists in my mind.

Nothing is more remarkable than the unanimity with which during the last few years the advanced world has put all its eggs in the basket of pragmatism, the basket that has been so alluringly garnished by Bergson's *Creative Evolution*. In this movement of thought Wells has inevitably become one of the leaders, and his practical desertion of the socialist cause is one of the main symptoms of it. The

creative energies of men, where society as a
whole is concerned, are, in this philosophy, conceived as bursting through the husks and institutions of the world, not consciously de-
stroying them but shedding them incidentally
and passing on. Now as regards sociology
there is an obvious fatalism in that; for the
burden of proof lies once more on a personal
basis, on a personal basis qualified by the capacity of the person. It is true that this creative and constructive tendency, like the total
tendency of modern life, is in the direction of
socialism, it is true that a thousand elements in
modern life which could never be engaged in
the class-war are led by it into line with socialism. Yet there capitalism is! Only the black-
browed Marxian steadily contemplates the fact
that year by year the rich compound their
riches and the poor their poverty, while those
that have no chance of creative outlets plant
dynamite.

I do not mean that Wells is "wrong" in
abandoning the economic for the psychological
approach,—that is plainly the inevitable course
for him. I wish simply to mark a distinction.

The gospel of Wells is an entirely personal
one; it frankly concerns itself with the inner
realities of the human mind, and in that lies
its great importance. But let us discriminate.
Like every purely personal doctrine it contains,
in relation to the facts and causes of society,
a certain quietism. It withdraws the mind from
corporate action and lays emphasis on corporate thought. But it recognizes no corporate
enemy. To be an opponent of capitalism as
such, is, in this philosophy, as quaint and crude
and crusty as to be an anti-suffragist or a
believer in politics (for it has become the
fashion to believe with fervor in the franchise
and scarcely to believe at all in what the franchise stands for).

There is then a certain danger in the creative
pragmatism of this particular time. If it actually does penetrate to the head men of the
world, if it is able to generate what I suppose
may be called a "moral equivalent" of duty—
and there is almost a probability that it will—
the hazard is won. If it does not—and many
keen thinkers and men of action are obdurate
—then we shall simply have the *fait accompli*

with compound interest. What if it should turn out in the end, after the best brains of socialism had all withdrawn from the economic programme of socialism, that capitalism grows all the greener in the sunlight of their tacit consent? There is Congress, there is Parliament, and there they propose to remain. Suppose they are not converted from the top? Is it altogether wise to stop persecuting them from the bottom?

So much before I pass on. This comment does not qualify the teaching of Wells. It merely supplements it from the economic side, and the supplement seems to me an important one.

Of a piece with his whole point of view is that he calls the right sociological method not a scientific but an artistic method: it consists of the making and comparing of Utopias. This idea he sets forth in his paper *The So-called Science of Sociology.* "What is called the scientific method," he says, "the method of observation, of theory about these observations, experiments in verification of that theory and confirmation or modification, really 'comes off'"

in the sciences in which the individuality of the
units can be pretty completely ignored." The
method that is all-important in the primary
physical sciences where the individuality of
atoms and molecules may conveniently be ignored for the sake of practical truth, becomes
in his view proportionately untrue as the sciences in their gradation approach the human
world. "We cannot," he says in *First and
Last Things,* "put humanity into a museum
and dry it for examination; our one still living specimen is all history, all anthropology,
and the fluctuating world of men. There is
no satisfactory means of dividing it and
nothing in the real world with which to compare it. We have only the remotest idea of its
'life-cycle' and a few relics of its origin and
dreams of its destiny." And in the paper I
have just mentioned he speaks of the Social
Idea as a thing "struggling to exist and realize itself in a world of egotisms, animals, and
brute matter. . . . Now I submit it is not
only a legitimate form of approach, but altogether the most promising and hopeful form
of approach, to endeavor to disentangle and

express one's personal version of that idea, and to measure realities from the standpoint of that realization. I think, in fact, that the creation of Utopias—and their exhaustive criticism—is the proper and distinctive method of sociology." This notion of sociology as properly artistic in method and diagnostic in aim indicates his main divergence from the methods and aims of Comte and Spencer.

And so one turns to his own illustration of this belief, *A Modern Utopia*. It is a beautiful Utopia, beautifully seen and beautifully thought; and it has in it some of that flavor of airy unrestraint one finds in *News from Nowhere*. Morris, of course, carries us into a world where right discipline has long since produced right will, so wholly and instinctively socialized that men can afford to be as free as anarchists would have the unsocialized men of our own time, a world such as Goethe had in mind when he said: "There is in man a force, a spring of goodness which counterbalances egoism; and if by a miracle it could for a moment suddenly be active in all men, the earth would at once be free from evil." Well, that is the miracle which has in some way just taken place before the curtain goes up on most Utopias; and I think that Wells has never been more skilful than in keeping this miracle quietly in his bag of tricks and devising meanwhile a plausible transition between us and that better world. It all happens in a moment and we are there. By an amazing legerdemain of logic he leaps the gap and presents us with a planet which at every point tallies with our own. It is a planet which does not contain a State but is a State, the flexible result of a free social gesture.

Mankind in the Making should be taken as introductory to *A Modern Utopia*. It is the sketch of a method towards attaining such a world state. It is a kind of treatise on education based on the assumption that "our success or failure with the unending stream of babies is the measure of our civilization." It opens with a complete repudiation of "scientific" breeding, as a scheme which ignores the uniqueness of individual cases and the heterogeneous nature of human ideals. "We are," says Wells, "not a bit clear what points to breed for, and what points to breed out;" while the interplay of strong and varied personalities we desire is contradictory to any uniform notions of beauty, capacity, and sanity, which thus cannot be bred for, so to speak, in the abstract. But in *A Modern Utopia* he outlines certain conditions limiting parentage, holding it necessary that in order to be a parent a man must be above a certain minimum of capacity and income, failing which he is indebted to the State for the keep of his children. Motherhood is endowed and becomes in this way a normal and remunerative career, which renders the mother capable of giving her time to the care and education of her children, as millions are not in a wage-earning civilization, and makes both her and her children independent of the ups and downs of her husband. His very detailed suggestions about the education of young children (illustrated also in *The Food of the Gods*) are at once a reminiscence of Rabelais and an anticipation of Madame Montessori. He insists upon uniform pronunciation (a very important matter in England, where diversity of language is one of the bulwarks of a rigid class-system), the universality and constant revision of text-books, the systematic reorganization of public library and bookselling methods, with a view to making the race think as a whole. He urges the necessity of rescuing literature from the accidents of the book-market by endowing critical reviews, chairs for the discussion of contemporary thought, and qualified thinkers and writers regardless of their special bias or principles. To strike a mean between the British abuse of government by hereditary privilege and the American abuse of government by electoral ma· chines he ingeniously proposes the election of officials by the jury method, twenty or thirty men being set aside by lot to determine the proper holders of office. And he is convinced of the importance in a democracy of abundant honors, privileges, even titles, and abundant opportunities for fruitful leisure.

I have already spoken of his belief that the right sociological method is the creation and comparison of individual Utopias. Thus his own free-hand sketch of a better world is, in fact, a criticism of all previous works of the kind. As distinguished from them the modern Utopia, he says, has to present not a finally perfect stage but a hopefully ascending one; it has to present men not as uniform types but as conflicting individualities with a common bond; and moreover it has to occupy, not some remote island or province "over the range" but a whole planet. The Utopia of Wells is a world which differs from the present world in one fundamental respect only—it has one initial advantage: that every individual in it has been *started right,* in the degree in which the collective knowledge of the world has rendered that possible.

But there is no need for me to say anything more about these books. They are the free and suggestive motions of a mind inexhaustibly fertile and given to many devices. Anyone who has read Wells at all is aware of his ingenuity, his equal capacity for large schemes and minute details, his truly Japanese belief in radical changes, once they are seen to be necessary and possible. And indeed the details of social arrangement follow naturally and profusely enough, once you get the frame of mind that wishes them. Wells in his Utopia presupposes the frame of mind. In short, he puts education first; he believes that the essential problems of the present are not economic but psychological.

And here where the constructive theory of Wells begins, let me quote a passage from *The New Machiavelli* that gives the gist of it:

The line of human improvements and the expansion of human life lies in the direction of education and finer initiatives. If humanity cannot develop an education far beyond anything that is now provided, if it cannot collectively invent devices and solve problems on a much richer, broader scale than it does at the present time, it cannot hope to achieve any very much finer order or any more general happiness than it now enjoys. We must believe, therefore, that it can develop such a training and education, or we must abandon secular constructive hope. And here my initial difficulty as against crude democracy comes in. If humanity at large is capable of that high education and those creative freedoms our hope demands, much more must its better and more vigorous types be so capable. And if those who have power and scope and freedom to respond to imaginative appeals cannot be won to the idea of collective self-development, then the whole of humanity cannot be won to that. From that one passes to what has become my general conception in politics, the conception of the constructive imagination working upon the vast complex of powerful people, enterprising people, influential people, amidst whom power is diffused to-day, to produce that self-conscious, highly selective, open-minded, devoted, aristocratic culture, which seems to me to be the necessary next phase in the development of human affairs. I see human progress, not as the spontaneous product of crowds of low minds swayed by elementary needs, but as a natural but elaborate result of intricate human interdependencies, of human energy and curiosity liberated and acting at leisure, of human passions and motives, modified and redirected by literature and art.

This permeation of the head men of the world, this creation of a natural collective-minded aristocracy appears now to be the permanent hope of Wells. It is the stuff of all his novels, it is the centre of his ethical system; and his *Utopia* is made possible by the existence in it of just such a flexible leading caste —the so-called Samurai. But before coming to the inner implications of this, to the individual and personal realities and difficulties of this, I must follow the development of the idea in Wells himself. At various times, in various works, he has presented it from a dozen different angles: as something that is certain to come, as something he greatly desires to come,

as something that will not come at all except
through prodigious effort, as something that
will come through a general catastrophe, as
something that will come through isolated individual endeavor, and the like. That is to say
he has presented his idea through all the various literary mediums of exposition, fable, pro-
phecy, psychological analysis, and ethical appeal.

It appears in a crude form in his first avow-
edly sociological work, *Anticipations*. He there
attempts to show that the chaos of society is of
itself beginning to generate a constructive
class, into whose hands it must ultimately fall.
The advance of mechanism, he predicts, will
produce four clearly defined classes: an immense shareholding class with all the potential-
ities of great property and a complete lack of
function with regard to that property; a non-
producing class of middle-men dependent on
these, and composed of agents, managers, lawyers, clerks, brokers, speculators, typists, and
organizers; the expropriated class of property-
less and functionless poor, whose present live-
lihood is dependent on the fact that machinery is not yet so cheap as their labor. And

amid this generally disorganized mass a fourth element will define itself. This in rudiment is the element of mechanics and engineers, whose work makes it necessary for them to understand the machines they are making and to be continually on the lookout for new methods. These men, he holds, will inevitably develop a common character based on a self-wrought scientific education and view of life. About them as a nucleus all the other skilled and constructive minds—doctors, teachers, investigators, writers, and the like—will tend to group themselves; and as the other classes in their very nature will tend to social disintegration, these will inevitably grow more and more conscious of a purpose, a reason, a function in common, and will disentangle themselves from the aimless and functionless masses about them. Democracy, as we know it, will meanwhile pass away. For democratic government unavoidably reduces itself to government by party machines and party machines depend for their existence on alarms, quarrelsome patriotisms, and international exasperations whose almost inevitable outcome is war.

Whether war follows or not, the power of society is bound to fall into the hands of the scientifically trained, constructive middle class, because this class is the only indispensable element in it. Without war this must occur just as soon as the spending and purchasing power of the shareholding class becomes dependent for its existence on the class which alone can save society from destruction. With war it will occur with even greater rapidity: for in the warfare of the future that nation is bound to win which has most effectively realized socialist ideals, in which the government can command, with least interference from private control, its roads, its food, its clothing, its material, its resources, which has most efficiently organized itself as a whole; and the class that modern warfare will bring to the front is the class that knows how to handle machinery and how to direct it. -But just as this class will be the most efficient in war, so will it be the most careful to prevent war: it will in fact confirm the ultimate tendency toward a World State at peace with itself, through the agency, not of any of the governments that we know to-day but of an informal coöperative organization which is altogether outside the governmental systems of society, and which may in time assimilate the greater part of the population of the world.

Such is the argument of this book, and except for the inevitability of it—the belief that all this *must* come to pass—Wells has not since abandoned it in any essential way. The new aristocracy that figures there, the advance-guard of a better civilization, is precisely the ethical ideal which is embodied in the chief characters of his novels. Thus too the Samurai of *A Modern Utopia* are figured as having arisen at first informally as the constructive minds disentangling themselves from the social chaos. Gradually becoming aware through research, discussion and coöperation of a common purpose, they have at last assumed a militant form and supplanted the political organizations of the world.

The general intention of all this finds utterance in the most poetic of all the fables of Wells, *The Food of the Gods*. The Food itself, invented by two undistinguished-looking scientists, becomes current in the world through the very haphazardness of a society which will not control discoveries detrimental to it and which consequently has no means of coping with a discovery capable of superseding it. "Heracleophorbia" has thus the same initial advantage as Tono-Bungay or any other shabby patent medicine. It has an additional advantage; for while patent medicines have the sanction of private enterprise and are controlled by secret patents for the gain of their inventors, the Food of the Gods, like every discovery of honorable scientists, is given freely to the world. Thus the Food and the gigantic race of supermen who spring from it and bring with them a nobler order of things are themselves generated by the very chaos they promise to supplant. Just in proportion as the inventors are frank and open men, having no secret gainful purpose, the Food spreads far and wide. It is stolen, spilled, scattered; and wherever it falls every living thing grows gigantic. Immense wasps drone like motor-cars over the meadows, chickens grow as large as emus, and here and there a baby fed upon it and unable thereafter to accept any less robust diet grows gradually to Rabelaisian proportions. Caddles, a type of all the growing giants, comes to his forty-foot maturity in a remote village where, as the mellow vicar observes, "Things change, but Humanity—*aere perennius.*" There he is taught by the little folk to submit himself to all his governors, teachers, spiritual pastors and masters and to order himself lowly and reverently to all his betters. They put him to work in the chalk-pits, where he learns to manage a whole quarry single-handed and makes of himself a rudimentary engineer, and then he breaks loose and tramps to London. He finds himself in the crowded New Kent Road, and they tell him he is obstructing the traffic: "But where is it going?" he says; "where does it come from? What does it mean?" Around him play the electric signs advertising Yanker's Yellow Pills and Tupper's Tonic Wine for Vigor, conveying to his troubled mind the significance of a world of chaos and accident, perverted instinct, and slavery to base suggestion.

Is it necessary to say that society becomes alarmed at last? Is it necessary to add that Wells opens fire upon it with his whole battery of satire? Plainly men and giants cannot live in the same world; the little men find their little ways, their sacred customs of order, home, and religion threatened by a strange new thing. The Children of the Food meanwhile have grown beyond the conventions and proportions of common life; they have experienced a kind of humanity to which all men can attain and from which there can be no retrogression to the lesser scheme. In the end, having found one another, they assemble in their embankment, the world against them. They sit amid their vast machinery, Titanic shapes in the darkness broken by searchlights and the flames of their forges. An ambassador from the old order brings them the terms upon which they may go free. They must separate themselves from the world and give up the Food. They refuse:

"Suppose we give up this thing that stirs within us," says the Giant Leaguer. . . . "What then? Will this little world of theirs be as it was before? They may fight against greatness in us who are the children of men, but can they conquer? . . . For greatness is abroad, and not only in us, not only in the Food, but in the purpose of all things! It is in the nature of all things, it is part of time and space. To grow and still to grow, from first to last, that is Being, that is the law of life."

CHAPTER IV

THE PHILOSOPHY OF THE NEW REPUBLICAN

IT is obvious that the socialism of Wells, touching as it does at every point the fabric of society, remains at bottom a personal and mystical conception of life. His typical socialist, or constructive man, or Samurai, or New Republican, or what you will, is as distinctly a poetic projection from life as Nietzsche's Superman, or Carlyle's Hero, or the Superior Man of Confucius. Like them, it implies a rule of conduct and a special religious attitude.

Nietzsche's Superman is a convenient figure by which for the moment to throw into relief the point I have in mind. Plainly a conception of this kind should never be intellectualized and defined. It is a living whole, as a human being is a living whole, and the only way to grasp it is to place oneself at the precise angle of the poet who conceived it. But the fixed intellect

of man is not often capable of rising to the
height of such an argument, nor do the run of
critics and interpreters rise to such a height
themselves. In the case of Nietzsche, particularly, they have confounded the confusion, urg-
ing precise definitions and at the same time dis-
agreeing among themselves as to which definitions may be held valid. But indeed the
Superman does not "mean" this or that: it can
merely be approached from different points of
view with different degrees of sympathy. And
so it is with the New Republican of Wells.

I have mentioned the Superman because
Wells himself has reached a conception of aristocracy similar in certain respects to that of
Nietzsche but in others wholly antagonistic. In
The Food of the Gods he certainly exhibits a
sympathy with Nietzsche on the poetical and
ideal side; for his giants are not simply grand-
children of Rabelais, they practise of necessity
a morality at variance with that of the little
men among whom they grow. When Caddles
comes to London he does not, and cannot, expect the little men to feed him; not intending
evil and seeing merely that he must live, he

sweeps the contents of a baker's shop into his
mouth with just the unconcerned innocence of
laws and prohibitions that a child would feel
before a blackberry bush. The very existence
of a larger, freer race implies a larger and
freer morality, and the giants and the little
folk alike see that the same world cannot for
long contain them both. But perhaps one can
mark the distinction by saying that, unlike the
Superman, they are not masters but servants
of the cosmic process. They themselves are
not the goal toward which the whole creation
tends. Humanity is not a setting for their
splendor, but something that wins through
them its own significance.

In fact it fully proves how profound is the
socialistic instinct in Wells, that though in
English wise and almost in the manner of Carlyle he has come to believe in the great ones of
this world, he has never lost the invincible socialist conviction that a great man is only a
figure of speech. In *The Discovery of the
Future* he says: "I must confess that I believe
that if by some juggling with space and time
Julius Cæsar, Napoleon, Edward IV, Wil-

liam the Conqueror, Lord Rosebery, and Rob-
ert Burns had all been changed at birth, it
would not have produced any serious disloca-
tion of the course of destiny. I believe that
these great men of ours are no more than
images and symbols and instruments taken, as
it were, haphazard by the incessant and consistent forces behind them." The individual
who stands on his achievement, the "lord of
creation," is to him at best a little misinformed,
at the worst blustering, dishonest, presuming,
absurd.

By an original instinct the Wells hero is an
inconspicuous little person, fastidiously unthe-
atrical, who cuts no figure personally and who,
to adopt a phrase from one of his later books,
"escapes from individuality in science and service." He abhors "personages." For the per-
sonage is one who, in some degree, stands on
his achievement, and to Wells man, both in his
love and his work, is experimental: he is an
experiment toward an impersonal synthesis,
the well-being of the species. It is true that
this idea of man as an experiment does not conflict with a very full development of personal-

ity. It consists in that; but personality to
Wells is attained purely through love and
work, and thus it comes to an end the moment
it becomes static, the moment one accepts the
laurel wreath, the moment one verges on self-
consequence.

The first published utterance of Wells was, I
think, a paper in *The Fortnightly Review* for
July, 1891, called *The Rediscovery of the
Unique*. It was one of the earliest of those
attacks on the logical approach to life, so char-
acteristic of contemporary thought: it stamped
him from the outset a pragmatist. The burden
of his argument was that since the investiga-
tions of Darwin it is no longer possible to ignore the uniqueness of every individual thing
in the universe and that "we only arrive at the
idea of similar beings by an unconscious or
deliberate disregard of an infinity of small
differences"—that, in brief, the method of
classification which is the soul of logic is untrue
to the facts of life. "Human reason," he
wrote, "in the light of what is being advanced,
appears as a convenient organic process based
on a fundamental happy misconception. . . .

The *raison d'être* of a man's mind is to avoid
danger and get food—so the naturalists tell us.
His reasoning powers are about as much a
truth-seeking tool as the snout of a pig, and he
may as well try to get to the bottom of things
by them as a mole might by burrowing."

I quote thus his rudely graphic early statement of the case, because he has not since sub-
stantially modified it and because it shows that
he already related it to human realities: and
indeed in the same paper he pointed out the relation that such an idea must bear to ordinary
conduct:

> Beings are unique, circumstances are unique, and
> therefore we cannot think of regulating our conduct by
> wholesale dicta. A strict regard for truth compels us
> to add that principles are wholesale dicta: they are sub-
> stitutes of more than doubtful value for an individual
> study of cases.

This conception of human reason as an altogether inadequate organ for getting at the
truth of things he later expanded in his Oxford lecture, *Scepticism of the Instrument;*
and, still further expanded, it forms the first
or metaphysical book of his *First and Last*

Things. It is unnecessary to discuss the
rights and wrongs of this primary point
in a generation familiar with James and
Bergson. It is an assumption of the purely
personal, experimental nature of truth which
has had a sufficient sanction of experience
greatly to modify contemporary practice in
ethics and sociology. And it should be noted
that Wells evolved it in his own study of physical science (a study serious enough to result in
text-books of Biology, Zoölogy, and Physi-
ography) and that he presents it, in accordance
with his own postulates, not as truth for everybody, but as his own personal contribution to
the sum of experience. The study of science
led him to see the limitations of the scientific
attitude, outside the primary physical sciences
which for practical purposes can afford to ignore individualities, in matters that approach
the world of human motives and affairs.

I do not propose to discuss this question of
logic. It is quite plain at least, as Wells observes, in the spirit of Professor James, that
"all the great and important beliefs by which
life is guided and determined are less of the

nature of fact than of artistic expression."
And therefore he is justified in proceeding as
follows:

> I make my beliefs as I want them. I do not attempt
> to go to fact for them. I make them thus and not thus
> exactly as an artist makes a picture so and not so. . . .
> That does not mean that I make them wantonly and re-
> gardless of fact. . . . The artistic method in this field
> of beliefs, as in the field of visual renderings, is one
> of great freedom and initiative and great poverty of
> test, that is all, but of no wantonness; the conditions of
> rightness are none the less imperative because they are
> mysterious and indefinable. I adopt certain beliefs be-
> cause I feel the need of them, because I feel an often
> quite unanalyzable rightness in them, because the alter-
> native of a chaotic life distresses me.

And this is the way in which he presents the
gist of his beliefs:

> I see myself in life as part of a great physical be-
> ing that strains and I believe grows toward Beauty, and
> of a great mental being that strains and I believe grows
> towards knowledge and power. In this persuasion that
> I am a gatherer of experience, a mere tentacle that ar-
> ranged thought beside thought for this Being of the Spe-
> cies, this Being that grows beautiful and powerful, in
> this persuasion I find the ruling idea of which I stand
> in need, the ruling idea that reconciles and adjudicates

among my warring motives. In it I find both concentration of myself and escape from myself, in a word, I find *Salvation.*

And again later:

The race flows through us, the race is the drama and we are the incidents. This is not any sort of poetical statement: it is a statement of fact. In so far as we are individuals, so far as we seek to follow merely individual ends, we are accidental, disconnected, without significance, the sport of chance. In so far as we realize ourselves as experiments of the species for the species, just in so far do we escape from the accidental and the chaotic. We are episodes in an experience greater than ourselves. . . . Now none of this, if you read me aright, makes for the suppression of one's individual difference, but it does make for its correlation. We have to get everything we can out of ourselves for this very reason that we do not stand alone; we signify as parts of a universal and immortal development. Our separate selves are our charges, the talents of which much has to be made. It is because we are episodical in the great synthesis of life that we have to make the utmost of our individual lives and traits and possibilities.

Naturally then, just as he holds by the existing State as a rudimentary collective organ in public affairs, so also, in theory, he holds by the existing Church. His Church of the Future bears to the existing Church just the relation which the ultimate State of socialism bears to the existing State. "The theory of a religion," says Wells, "may propose the attainment of Nirvana or the propitiation of an irascible Deity or a dozen other things as its end and aim. The practical fact is that it draws together great multitudes of diverse individualized people in a common solemnity and self-subordination, however vague, and is so far like the State, and in a manner far more intimate and emotional and fundamental than the State, a synthetic power. And in particular the idea of the Catholic Church is charged with synthetic suggestion; it is in many ways an idea broader and finer than the constructive idea of any existing State."

All of which I take to be very much the position of Erasmus face to face with Luther and of Matthew Arnold face to face on the one hand with Nonconformity and on the other with Darwinism: that the Church is a social fact greater in importance than any dogmatic system it contains. To Wells any sort of vol-

untary self-isolation, any secession from anything really synthetic in society, is a form of
"sin." And like many Catholics he justifies a
certain Machiavelism in squaring one's personal doubts with the collective end. Thus he
holds that test oaths and declarations of formal
belief are of the same nature as the oath of al-
legiance a republican takes to the King, petty
barriers that cannot weigh against the good
that springs from placing oneself *en rapport*
with the collective religious consciousness; at
least in the case of national Churches, which
profess to represent the whole spiritual life of
a nation and which cannot therefore be regarded as exclusive to any affirmative religious
man. The individual, he says, must examine
his special case and weigh the element of
treachery against the possibility of coöperation; as far as possible he must repress his private tendency toward social fragmentation,
hold fast to the idea of the Church as essentially
a larger fact than any specific religious beliefs,
and work within it for the recognition of this
fact. I have mentioned Catholic reasoning;
Wells appears to be in general agreement with

Newman as to the subordination of private intellectual scruples to the greater unity of faith.

But indeed I doubt if it is fair to take him too much at his word in specific matters of this kind. *First and Last Things* has that slightly official quality which goes with all Confessions of Faith out loud. If his intention has led him to square himself with lines of thought and conduct where, to speak the truth, he is an alien, his intention remains, and that is plain and fine.

The synthetic motive gains its very force through the close-knitting of keenly-developed, proud, and valiant individualities. In Wells the synthetic motive and the individual motive qualify and buttress one another; and he is quite as much opposed to the over-predominance of the synthetic motive where the personal motive is deficient as he is to the self-indulgence of the purely personal life. Thus the Assembly in *A Modern Utopia* is required to contain a certain number of men outside the Samurai class, because, as they explain, "there is a certain sort of wisdom that comes of sin and laxness, which is necessary to the perfect ruling of life," and their Canon contains a prayer "to save the world from unfermented men." So also in *First and Last Things* Wells remarks: "If I were a father confessor I should begin my catalogue of sins by asking, 'Are you a man of regular life?' and I would charge my penitent to go away forthwith and commit some practicable saving irregularity; to fast or get drunk or climb a mountain or sup on pork and beans or give up smoking or spend a month with publicans and sinners." Plainly his collective purpose is nothing unless it consists of will, will even to wilfulness, even to perversity.

And this leads one back to that early assertion of his that since beings and circumstances are unique, we must get rid of the idea that conduct should be regulated by general principles. Similarly, at the outset of *Mankind in the Making* he says it is necessary "to reject and set aside all abstract, refined, and intellectualized ideas as starting propositions, such ideas as Right, Liberty, Happiness, Duty, or Beauty, and to hold fast to the assertion of the fundamental nature of life as a tissue and succession of births." Goodness and Beauty, he says, cannot be considered apart from good and beautiful things and one's personal notions of the good and beautiful have to be determined by one's personal belief about the meaning of life. Thus, to take an illustration from his novels, one of the most odious traits of such a father as Ann Veronica's or Mr. Pope in *Marriage* is that they wish to regulate their daughters, not by a study of what is and must be good in their eyes, but by a general sweeping view of what good daughters ought to be.

Now since his own idea of the purpose of life is the development of the collective consciousness of the race, his idea of the Good is that which contributes to this synthesis, and the Good Life is that which, as he says, "most richly gathers and winnows and prepares experience and renders it available for the race, that contributes most effectively to the collective growth." And as a corollary to this, Sin is essentially "the service of secret and personal ends." The conflict in one way or another between this Good and this Evil forms the substance of each of the main group of his novels.

Aside from the novels of shop-life, each of his principal men begins life with a passionate and disinterested ambition to gather and prepare experience and render it available for the race; each one falls from this ambition to the service of secret and personal ends. Lewisham, Capes, Ponderevo, Remington, Trafford are, each in his own way, human approximations, with all the discount of actual life, of the ethical standard of Wells himself as it is generalized in the New Republicans and the Samurai. They illustrate how fully the socialism of Wells is summed up in a conception of character.

But before turning to the actual men and women who form the substance of his novels, I must add something about those wraith-like beings, the Samurai of *A Modern Utopia,* which fully embody his ideal.

The name Samurai, to begin with, is not a random choice, for it is plain that the Japanese temper is akin to that of Wells. The career of the Japanese as a nation during the last fifty years perfectly illustrates his frequent contention that in modern warfare success falls to the nation that has most completely realized the socialistic, as distinguished from the individualistic, notion of society. "Behind her military capacity is the disciplined experience of a thousand years," says Lafcadio Hearn, who proceeds to show at what cost, in everything we are apt to regard as human, this disciplined power has been achieved—the cost of individual privacy in rights, property, and conduct.

But aside from social ideals and achievements one instinctively feels that Wells likes Japanese human nature. In one of his early essays, long since out of print, he remarks:

I like my art unadorned; thought and skill and the other strange quality that is added thereto to make things beautiful—and nothing more. A farthing's worth of paint and paper, and behold! a thing of beauty!—as they do in Japan. And if it should fall into the fire—well, it has gone like yesterday's sunset, and to-morrow there will bc another.

He contrasts this with the ordinary English view of art and property, mahogany furniture and "handsome" possessions:

The pretence that they were the accessories to human life was too transparent. *We* werc the accessories;

we minded them for a little while, and then we passed away. They wore us out and cast us aside. We were the changing scenery; they were the actors who played on through the piece.

There is no Being but Becoming is the special dictum of Wells, a dictum which does not consort with mahogany sideboards, but is tangibly expressed in Japanese architecture. And if Wells naturally likes Japanese art, its economy, delicacy, ephemerality, its catlike nicety, its paucity of color, its emphasis of design, its "starkness," it is plain also that many qualities of the Japanese character must also appeal irresistibly to him: the light hold they have on all those things into which one settles down, from stolid leather armchairs to comfortable private fortunes; their lack of self-consequence, their alertness, their athletic freedom from everything that encumbers, their remoteness from port-wine and *embonpoint*. These things exist in Wells's notion of right human nature.

Thus the Samurai. They are delegates of the species, experimenting and searching for new directions; they instinctively view themselves as explorers for the race, as disinterested agents. And their own self-development on this disinterested basis is not only the purpose of their own lives, but also the method by which the Life Impulse discovers and records itself and pushes on to ever wider and richer manifestations.

The socialism of Wells is merely a building out from this conception. He is persuaded that this kind of experimental exercise is not simply a happy indulgence for the few fortunately placed, but that it is actually virtue and the only virtue. And this notion of personal virtue—personal in quality, social in effect—once conceded, it follows that the moulding of life must proceed with reference to this.

Chapter V

HUMAN NATURE

THERE is always a certain disadvantage
in approaching human nature through a
theory or in the light of an ideal. If I am
doing that, it is my own fault and by no means
the fault of Wells. He has himself abandoned
socialism, in the ordinary sense of the term, because it has too much of the *à priori* about it;
he has abandoned economics because it deals
with man as a mass-mind; he has come to rest
in human nature itself and he has made his
theories subject to human nature.

"All fables, indeed, have their morals; but
the innocent enjoy the story," says Thoreau.
Most readers of the novels of Wells, I suppose,
have no notion that a theory of life runs
through them and unites them. And they are
right. The force of a work of art does not
reside in its "inner meanings." An admirable
work of art will always no doubt possess "inner

meanings" in plenty and the unhappy mind of
man will always rout them out. But to separate the intellectual structure of anything from
the thing itself is just like any other kind of
vivisection: you expose the brain and you kill
the dog. A work of art is a moving living
whole that speaks to the moving living whole
which is oneself. We are insensibly modified
by reading as by other experience. We come
to feel differently, see differently, act differently. Without doubt Wells has altered the
air we breathe and has made a conscious fact
in many minds the excellence that resides in
certain types of men and modes of living and
the odiousness that resides in others. Socialism, like everything else which changes the
world, comes as a thief in the night.

Still, it is plain that Wells himself began
with doctrine foremost; richness of experience
has led him only after many years to get the
horse before the cart. From the first he was
aware of a point of view—it was the point of
view, writ large, of his own self-made career,
growing gradually more and more coherent.
Throughout his romances, down to the very

end, his chief interest was theoretical rather than human. Only this can account for the violent wrenching of life and character in them to suit the requirements of a predetermined idea. The Food of the Gods, for example, is so far the essential fact of the book that bears its name that the characters in this book are merely employed to give the Food a recognizable human setting. Throughout his romances, indeed, men exist for inventions, not inventions for men.

Yet the "human interest," as it is called, was there from the outset, side by side with this main theoretic interest in the scientific and socialistic possibilities of life. The series of novels began almost as early as the series of romances. Two "streams of tendency" run side by side throughout the earlier writings of Wells—streams of tendency which meet fully for the first time in *Tono-Bungay,* and have formed a single main current in the novels subsequent to that. On the one hand was the stream of constructive theory, not yet brought into contact with human nature, on the other the stream of "human interest," not yet brought into contact with constructive theory. Mr. Hoopdriver, of *The Wheels of Chance,* and Kipps, are typical of this earlier fiction, specimens of muddled humanity as such, one might say, quite unmitigated by the train of thought, the possibility of doing something *with* muddled humanity, which was growing more and more urgent in the romances.

In *Tono-Bungay,* as I have said, one sees the union of these two trains of interest, muddled humanity being represented in Uncle Ponderevo, constructive theory in George Ponderevo. And in all the subsequent novels this fusion continues. The background in each case is the static world of muddle from which Wells is always pushing off into the open sea of possibilities, the foreground being occupied by a series of men and women who represent this dynamic forward movement. And the philosophy of Wells has finally come to port in human nature.

"Few modern socialists," he says somewhere, "present their faith as a complete panacea, and most are now setting to work in earnest upon those long-shirked preliminary problems of

human interaction through which the vital
problem of a collective head and brain can
alone be approached." And elsewhere he says:
"Our real perplexities are altogether psychological. There are no valid arguments against
a great-spirited socialism but this, that people
will not. Indolence, greed, meanness of spirit,
the aggressiveness of authority, and above all
jealousy, jealousy from pride and vanity, jealousy for what we esteem our possessions, jealousy for those upon whom we have set the
heavy fetters of our love, a jealousy of criticism and association, these are the real obstacles
to those brave large reconstructions, those
profitable abnegations and brotherly feats of
generosity that will yet turn human life—of
which our individual lives are but the momen-
tary parts—into a glad, beautiful and tri-
umphant coöperation all round this sunlit
world."

Inevitably then he sees the world as divided
roughly into two worlds, and human nature as
of two general kinds. There is the static
world, the normal, ordinary world which is on
the whole satisfied with itself, together with

the great mass of men who compose and sanction it; and there is the ever-advancing better world, pushing through this outworn husk in the minds and wills of creative humanity. In one of his essays he has figured this opposition as between what he calls the Normal Social Life and the Great State. And in one of those *dégagé* touch-and-go sketches in which he so often sums up the history of humankind, he has presented the Normal Social Life as a "common atmosphere of cows, hens, dung, toil, ploughing, economy, and domestic intimacy," an immemorial state of being which implies on the part of men and women a perpetual acquiescence—a satisfied or hopeless consent—to the end of time. But as against this normal conception of life he points out that modern circumstances have developed in men, through machinery, the division of labor, etc., a "surplus life" which does not fit into the Normal scheme at all, and that humanity has returned "from a closely tethered to a migratory existence." And he observes: "The history of the immediate future will, I am convinced, be very largely the history of the conflict of the needs of this new population with the institutions, the boundaries, the laws, prejudices, and deep-rooted traditions established during the home-keeping, localized era of mankind's career."

Two conceptions of life, two general types of character, two ethical standards are here set in opposition, and this opposition is maintained throughout the novels of Wells. Thus on the title-page of *The New Machiavelli* appears the following quotation from Professor James: "It suffices for our immediate purpose that tender-minded and tough-minded people . . . do both exist." In *A Modern Utopia* this division appears typically in the two men from our world who play off against one another, the botanist and the narrator of the story. The "tender-mindedness" of the botanist is exhibited in the fact that he cares nothing for a better world if it is to deprive him of the muddled, inferior and sentimental attachments of his accustomed life, and prefers them to the austerer, braver prospect that is offered him. "Tough-mindedness," on the other hand, is above all the state of living, not

in one's attachments, habits, possessions, not in
the rut of least resistance, but in the sense of
one's constructive and coöperative relationship
to the whole sum of things, in being "a conscious part of that web of effort and per-
plexity which wraps about our globe." And
indeed the constant theme of the novels of
Wells might be described as tough-mindedness
with lapses.

For the heroes of Wells do lapse: they pay
that tribute to "human nature" and the overwhelming anti-social forces in the world and
in man himself. They fall, as a rule, from
"virtue" to the service of secret and personal
ends. *Cherchez la femme.* Mr. Lewisham, in-
sufficiently prepared and made to feel that society does not want him, has to give up his
disinterested ambitions in science and scramble
for money to support a wife whom instinct has
urged him, however imprudently, to marry.
George Ponderevo gives up science and is
forced into abetting his uncle's patent medicine enterprise for the same reason. For the
same reason, too, Capes takes to commercial
play-writing to support Ann Veronica; and to

stand behind the extravagance of Marjorie,
Trafford, having discovered in his researches
an immensely valuable method of making arti-
ficial india-rubber which he is going to make
public for the use of society, is persuaded to
compromise his honor as a scientist and monop-
olize his discovery for private gain. In *Tono-
Bungay* the enterprise is a swindling patent
medicine, which many business men would refuse to have anything to do with; but in *Marriage* the proposition belongs to what is called
"legitimate business," and it may be well to
quote a passage to show the subtlety and, at
the same time, from this point of view, the very
substantial nature of temptation and sin:

Solomonson had consulted Trafford about this matter at Vevey, and had heard with infinite astonishment
that Trafford had already roughly prepared and was
proposing to complete and publish, unpatented and absolutely unprotected, first a smashing demonstration of
the unsoundness of Behren's claim and then a lucid exposition of just what had to be done and what could
be done to make an india-rubber absolutely indistin-
guishable from the natural product. The business man
could not believe his ears.

"My dear chap, positively—you mustn't!" Solomonson had screamed. . . . "Don't you see all you are throwing away?"

"I suppose it's our quality to throw such things away," said Trafford. . . . "When men dropped that idea of concealing knowledge, alchemist gave place to chemist, and all that is worth having in modern life, all that makes it better and safer and more hopeful than the ancient life began."

"My dear fellow," said Solomonson, "I know, I know. But to give away the synthesis of rubber! To just shove it out of the window into the street!" . . . Everything that had made Trafford up to the day of his marriage was antagonistic to such strategic reservations. The servant of science has as such no concern with personal consequences; his business is the steady relentless clarification of knowledge. The human affairs he changes, the wealth he makes or destroys, are no concern of his; once these things weigh with him, become primary, he has lost his honor as a scientific man.

"But you *must* think of consequences," Solomonson had cried during those intermittent talks at Vevey. "Here you are, shying this cheap synthetic rubber of yours into the world—for it's bound to be cheap! anyone can see that—like a bomb into a market-place. What's the good of saying you don't care about the market-place, that *your* business is just to make bombs and drop them out of the window? You smash up things just the same. Why! you'll ruin hundreds and thousands of people, people living on rubber shares, people working in plantations, old, inadaptable workers in rubber works. . . ."

"I believe we can do the stuff at tenpence a pound," said Solomonson, leaning back in his chair at last. . . . "So soon, that is, as we deal in quantity. Tenpence! We can lower the price and spread the market, sixpence by sixpence. In the end—there won't be any more plantations. Have to grow tea."

There we have Eve and the apple brought up to date, sin being the choice of a private and individual good at the expense of the general good. The honor of a doctor or a scientist consists in not concealing and monopolizing discoveries. But why should the line be drawn at doctors and scientists? There is the crux of socialist ethics.

By this type of compromise the actual New Republicans fall short of their Utopian selves, the Samurai. But compromise is well within the philosophy of Wells. "The individual case," he says in *First and Last Things,* "is almost always complicated by the fact that the existing social and economic system is based upon conditions that the growing collective intelligence condemns as unjust and undesirable, and that the constructive spirit in men now seeks to supersede. We have to live in a pro-

visional state while we dream of and work for
a better one." And elsewhere: "All socialists
everywhere are like expeditionary soldiers far
ahead of the main advance. The organized
State that should own and administer their
possessions for the general good has not ar-
rived to take them over; and in the meanwhile
they must act like its anticipatory agents according to their lights and make things ready
for its coming."

But if the New Republican is justified in
compromising himself for the means of sub-
sistence, how much more in the matter of love!
"All for love, and the world well lost" might
be written over several of Wells's novels. But,
in reality, is the world lost at all under these
conditions? On the contrary, it is gained, and
the more unconsciously the better, in babies.
Love belongs to the future and the species with
more finality than the greatest constructive
work of the present, and the heroines of Wells
are inordinately fond of babies. When Schopenhauer analyzed the metaphysics of love he
showed that natural selection is a quite inevitable thing seeking its own. In Wells love is

equally irresistible and direct. Whenever it appears in his books it makes itself unmistakably known, and, having done so, it cuts its way straight to its consummation, through every obstacle of sentiment, affection, custom, and conventionality. It is as ruthless as the Last Judgment, and like the Last Judgment it occurs only once.

Why then does it appear promiscuous? The answer to this question refers one back to the underlying contention of Wells that there are two kinds of human beings and two corresponding ethics, and that in the end the New Republican who has become aware of himself cannot consort with the Normal Social breed. But in actual life this standard becomes entangled with many complexities. Just as, in a world of commercial competition, it is the lot of most of those who try to give themselves whole-heartedly to disinterested work that they place themselves at such a disadvantage as ultimately to have to make a choice between work and love, so the pressure of society and the quality of human nature itself create entanglements of every kind. It is the nature of life that one grows only gradually to the secure sense of a personal aim, and that meanwhile day by day one has given hostages to fortune. To wake up and find oneself suddenly the master of a purpose is without doubt, in the majority of cases, to find oneself mortgaged beyond hope to the existing fact. The writer who sets out to make his way temporarily and as a stepping-stone by journalism finds himself in middle age with ample means to write what he wishes to write only to find also that he has become for good and all—a journalist! And so it is with lovers. Only in the degree to which free will remains a perpetual and present faith can "love and fine thinking" remain themselves; free of their attachments, free of their obligations, and mortgages, and discounts. That is the quality of a decent marriage, and the end of a marriage that is not decent.

It is no business of mine to justify the sexual ethics of Wells. But there is a difference between a fact and an intention, and what I have just said serves to explain the intention. Consider, in the light of it, a few of his characters, both in and out of marriage. Ann Veronica from the first frankly owns that she is not in love with Manning, but every kind of social hypnotism is brought into motion to work on her ignorance of life and to confuse her sense of free-will. George Ponderevo simply outgrows Marion; but you cannot expect him not to grow, and who is responsible for the limited, furtive, second-hand world in which Marion has lived and which has irrevocably moulded her? Margaret's world, too, is a second-hand world, though on a socially higher plane: she lives in a pale dream of philanthropy and Italian art, shocked beyond any mutual understanding by everything that really belongs in the first-hand world of her husband. These characters meet and pass one another like moving scales; they never stand on quite the same plane. And then the inevitable always occurs. For, just as the Children of the Food cannot consort with the little folk they promise to supersede, so it appears to be a fixed part of the programme of Wells that New Republicans can only love other New Republicans with success.

He implies this indeed in *A Modern Utopia:*

"A man under the Rule who loves a woman who
does not follow it, must either leave the Samurai to
marry her, or induce her to accept what is called the
Woman's Rule, which, while it exempts her from the
severer qualifications and disciplines, brings her regi-
men into a working harmony with his."
"Suppose she breaks the Rule afterwards?"
"He must leave either her or the order."
"There is matter for a novel or so in that."
"There has been matter for hundreds."

Wells has written six himself. *Love and
Mr. Lewisham, Ann Veronica, Tono-Bungay,
The New Machiavelli, Marriage, The Passionate Friends,* are all variations on this
theme. In one of these alone life's double motive succeeds in establishing itself, and it is for
this reason that *Marriage,* to my thinking the
weakest of his novels from an artistic point of
view, is the most important concrete presenta-
tion of the philosophy of Wells. It is an inferior book, but it gives one the sense of a
problem solved. By passing through a necessary yet feasible discipline, Trafford and Marjorie bridge over the gap between haphazard

human nature and the better nature of socialism, and become Samurai in fact.

These entanglements of the actual world
would be an overwhelming obstacle to a socialism less vigorous than that of Wells. But
obstacles give edge to things, and for a man
who loves order no one could have pictured disorder with more relish than he. Only a pure
theorist could regret the artistic zest with
which he portrays our muddled world. Running amuck was a constant theme in his early
writings; his comets ran amuck, and so did Mr.
Bessel, and there is no more relished wanton
scene than that of the Invisible Man running
amuck through the Surrey villages. Inten-
tionally or not, this relish in disorder reinforces
the prime fact about his view of order. He abhors the kind of order which is often ignorant-
ly confounded with the socialist aim, the order
which classifies and standardizes. He desires
a collective consciousness only through the exercise of a universally unimpeded free will,
and he would rather have no collectiveness at
all than one that implies the sacrifice of this
free will. He wishes to work only on the most

genuine human stuff. This was the basis of
his break with the Fabian Society; it is the basis of his dislike of bureaucratic methods which
deprive people of beer when they want beer.
It defines his notion of the true method of socialism as first of all an education of the human will toward voluntary right discipline.

His appeal, then, is a personal one. He has
proved this indeed by his repudiation of all attempts to embody in practice his proposed order of voluntary nobility, the Samurai. Certain groups of young people actually organized themselves upon the Rule that he had outlined, and it was this that led him to see how
entirely his ideal had been personal and artistic
rather than practical. Anyone at all familiar
with religious history and psychology will see
how inevitably any such group would tend to
emphasize the Rule and the organization rather
than the socially constructive spirit for which
the whole was framed, and how the organization would itself separate from the collective
life of the world and become a new sect among
the many sects. It was the same instinct that
led Emerson, Transcendental communist as

he was, to look askance at Brook Farm. It has
been the want of an equal tact in eminent religious minds that has made society a warfare
of sect and opinion.

When one tries to focus the nature of his appeal one recalls a passage in one of his books
where he sums up the ordinary mind of the
world and the function which all socialism
bears to this mind:

> It is like a very distended human mind; it is without
> a clear aim; it does not know except in the very vaguest
> terms what it wants to do; it has impulses, it has fan-
> cies; it begins and forgets. In addition, it is afflicted
> with a division within itself that is strictly analogous to
> that strange mental disorder which is known to psy-
> chologists as multiple personality. It has no clear con-
> ception of the whole of itself, it goes about forgetting
> its proper name and address. Part of it thinks of itself
> as one great thing, as, let us say, Germany; another
> thinks of itself as Catholicism, another as the white
> race, or Judæa. At times one might deem the whole
> confusion not so much a mind as incurable dementia—
> a chaos of mental elements, haunted by invincible and
> mutually incoherent fixed ideas. . . . In its essence
> the socialistic movement amounts to this: it is an attempt
> in this warring chaos of a collective mind to pull itself
> together, to develop and establish a governing idea of

itself. It is the development of the collective self-consciousness of humanity.

Certainly the road to this can only be through a common understanding. The willing and unwilling servitudes of men, the institutions of society that place love and work in opposition to one another, the shibboleths of party, the aggressive jingoisms of separate peoples, the immemorial conspiracy by which men have upheld the existing fact, these things do spring from the want of imagination, the want of energetic faith, the want of mutual understanding. To this inner and personal problem Wells has applied himself. Can life be ventilated, can the mass of men be awakened to a sense of those laws of social gravitation and the transmutation of energy by which life is proved a myriad-minded organism, can the ever-growing sum of human experience and discovery clear up the dark places within society and within man? Among those who have set themselves to the secular solution of these questions—and I am aware of the limits of any secular solution—there are few as effective as Wells.

Consider him in relation to a single concrete issue, the issue of militarism:

> Expenditure upon preparation for war falls, roughly, into two classes: there is expenditure upon things that have a diminishing value, things that grow old-fashioned and wear out, such as fortifications, ships, guns, and ammunition, and expenditure upon things that have a permanent and even growing value, such as organized technical research, military and naval experiment, and the education and increase of a highly trained class of war experts.

And in *The Common Sense of Warfare* he urges a lavish expenditure on "education and training, upon laboratories and experimental stations, upon chemical and physical research and all that makes knowledge and leading." Separate the principle involved here from the issue it is involved in, get the intention clear of the fact, and you find that he is saying just the better sort of things that Matthew Arnold said. Militarism granted, are you going to do military things or are you going to make military things a stepping-stone toward the clarification of thought, the training of men, the develop-

ment of race-imagination? Militarism has
been to a large extent the impetus that has
made the Germans and the Japanese the
trained, synthetic peoples they are. And these
very qualities are themselves in the end hostile
to militarism. Militarism considered in this
sense is precisely what the General Strike is in
the idea of M. Georges Sorel: a myth, a thing
that never comes to pass, but which trains the
general will by presenting it with a concrete
image toward which the will readily directs itself. Kipling, in the eyes of the New Machiavelli, at least made the nation aware of what
comes

> All along o' dirtiness, all along o' mess,
> All along o' doing things rather more or less.

There is in this no defence of militarism.
Granting the facts of society, there is a way
that accepts and secures them as they are and
another way of turning them into the service
of the future, and a people that has trained
itself with reference to a particular issue has
virtually trained itself for all issues.

But no one, I think, has measured the diffi-

culties of real progress more keenly than Wells
has come to measure them. The further he has
penetrated into human nature the more alive
he has become to these difficulties. *The New
Machiavelli* is a modern *Rasselas* that has no
happy valley in the end, and Remington
passes from party to party, penetrating in-
ward from ideas to the better stuff of mankind, hoping to embody his "white passion of
statecraft," and in the end demonstrating to
himself the futility of all groups and parties
alike.

And as with parties, so with men. Consider that scene in *The Passionate Friends* where
Stratton tries to explain in writing to his
father what he has been experiencing and why
he must go away. He writes page after page
without expressing himself and at last, certain
that he and his father cannot come into touch,
sends off a perfunctory note and receives a
perfunctory reply. "There are times," he
adds, "when the inexpressiveness of life comes
near to overwhelming me, when it seems to me
we are all asleep or entranced, and but a little
way above the still cows who stand munching

slowly in a field. . . . Why couldn't we and why didn't we talk together!"

That is the burden of his latest novel. By this touchstone he has come to measure the possibility of that openness of mind, that mutual understanding, that ventilation of life and thought through which alone the Great State can exist.

Chapter VI

A PERSONAL CHAPTER

I DOUBT if there are many living men of note who, a generation after they are dead, will be so fully and easily "explained" as H. G. Wells. He is a most personal and transparent writer, he is the effect of conditions and forces which have existed for scarcely more than two generations. But for these very reasons it is very difficult to see him in perspective, and to explain him would be to explain the age in which we live. Let me at least give certain facts and reflections about his life written by Wells himself, a few years ago, in the introduction to a Russian translation of his writings:

I was born * in that queer indefinite class that we call in England the middle class. I am not a bit aristocratic; I do not know any of my ancestors beyond

*September 21, 1866.

my grandparents, and about them I do not know very much, because I am the youngest son of my father and mother and their parents were all dead before I was born. My mother was the daughter of an innkeeper at a place called Midhurst, who supplied post-horses to the coaches before the railways came; my father was the son of the head gardener of Lord de Lisle at Penshurst Castle, in Kent. They had various changes of fortune and position; for most of his life my father kept a little shop in a suburb of London, and eked out his resources by playing a game called cricket, which is not only a pastime, but a show which people will pay to see, and which, therefore, affords a living to professional players. His shop was unsuccessful, and my mother, who had been a lady's maid, became, when I was twelve years old, housekeeper in a large country house. I too was destined to be a shopkeeper. I left school at thirteen for that purpose. I was apprenticed first to a chemist, and, that proving unsatisfactory, to a draper. But after a year or so it became evident to me that the facilities that were and still are increasing in England offered me better chances in life than a shop and comparative illiteracy could do; and so I struggled for and got various grants and scholarships that enabled me to study and take a degree in science and some mediocre honors in the new and now great and growing University of London. . . . After I had graduated I taught biology for two or three years, and then became a journalist. . . . I began first to write literary articles, criticisms, and so forth, and presently short imaginative stories in which I made use of the teeming suggestions of modern science. . . .

So much for the facts. The reflections are not less illuminating:

The literary life is one of the modern forms of adventure. Success with a book—even such a commercially modest success as mine has been—means in the English-speaking world not merely a moderate financial independence, but the utmost freedom of movement and intercourse. A poor man is lifted out of his narrow circumstances into familiar and unrestrained intercourse with a great variety of people. He sees the world; if his work excites interest, he meets philosophers, scientific men, soldiers, artists, professional men, politicians of all sorts, the rich, the great, and he may make such use of them as he can. He finds himself no longer reading in books and papers, but hearing and touching at first hand the big questions that sway men, the initiatives that shape human affairs. . . . To be a literary artist is to want to render one's impressions of the things about one. Life has interested me enormously and filled me with ideas and associations I want to present again. I have liked life and like it more and more. The days in the shop and the servants' hall, the straitened struggles of my early manhood, have stored me with vivid memories that illuminate and help me to appreciate all the wider vistas of my later social experiences. I have friends and intimates now at almost every social level, from that of a peer to that of a pauper, and I find my sympathies and curiosities stretching like a thin spider's web from top to bottom of the social tangle. I count that wide social range one of the most fortunate accidents of my life, and another is that I am of a diffident and ineffectual presence, unpunctual, fitful, and easily bored by other than literary effort; so that I am not tempted to cut a figure in the world and abandon that work of observing and writing which is my proper business in it.

This candid and exact statement enables us to see just how far, in matters of fact, experience and belief, the autobiographical motive has entered his writings. It would be possible to show how inevitably such an ideal as that of the New Republican Samurai arose from such a life; how much that conscious and deliberate insistence on personal efficiency and orderly ways, that repudiation of mental confusion, sluggishness, and sentiment may figure as a kind of stepping-stone from the world of Kipps and Polly to the world of Remington and Trafford; how a self-wrought scientific education would form the basis of an ideal of aristocracy rising from it; and how the motto "There is no Being but Becoming" would express its own constant desertion of levels

achieved, its own pressing upward to levels
equally transient.   Just as the "democratic
person" of Whitman raises his own fervent,
chaotic, and standardless experience into an
ideal, so also the ideal of Wells is nothing else
than the projection of his own experimental
opportunism.   It is impossible in discussing
Wells to ignore this social ascent; for in England a man passes from one stratum to another
only by virtue of a certain lack of substantial-
ity, a power to disencumber himself, to shed
customs and affections and all the densenesses
and coagulations which mark each grade in
that closely defined social hierarchy.   The
world of shopkeeping in England is a world
girt about with immemorial subjections; it is,
one might say, a moss-covered world; and to
shake oneself loose from it is to become a roll-
ing stone, a drifting and unsettled, a detached
and acutely personal, individual.   It is to pass
from a certain confined social maturity, a confused mellowness, into a world wholly adventurous and critical, into a freedom which
achieves itself at the expense of solidity and
warmth.   In Wells, for instance, the sense of

the soil is wholly supplanted by the sense of machinery. His evolution has been the reverse of the usual evolution from what Bacon called the *lumen siccum* to the *lumen humidum,* from the dry light to the light that is drenched in customs and affections. Instead of growing mellower, he has grown more and more fluid and electric, in direct ratio to the growing width of his social horizon.

To prove this one has only to consider his novels. There was a time when he had in common with Dickens and De Foe the quality they have in common with one another—the quality of homeliness. He drew the little world he knew well, the limited and lovable world of small folk. Mr. Hoopdriver, Delia the chambermaid, Kipps and Ann Pornick—a score of these helpless, grown-up little children he pictured with a radiant affection, tempering the wind to the shorn lamb. It is more in the nature of his later thought to see poverty as a wasteful rather than a cruel thing, even though he may not have approached the harsh realism of Bernard Shaw's observation: "I have never had any feeling about the English working

classes except a desire to abolish them and re-
place them by sensible people."

Certainly he has not experienced any other
world in quite this way. "I count that wide
social range one of the most fortunate accidents in my life," he says. Accidental one feels
it to be, as of a man inhabiting the great world
by virtue of sheer talent, whose nature has not
in any sense settled there. His philosophy and
his socialism are outgrowths of his own experience; they erect into reasons and theories the
nature of a life which is not at home, and which
easily unburdens itself of all that seems insen-
sate because it is unfamiliar. To be a socialist at
all is to have accustomed oneself, through necessity or imagination, to a certain detachment
from a great many of the familiar, lovable, en-
cumbering, delightful stupidities of the world.
And Wells has travelled up and down through
time and space too much to have any great regard for the present. "I have come to be, I
am afraid," he says, in *The Future in America,*
"even a little insensitive to fine immediate
things through this anticipatory habit. . . .
There are times indeed when it makes life seem

so transparent and flimsy, seem so dissolving, so passing on to an equally transitory series of consequences——." His hold upon the present is so far from inevitable that *The New Machiavelli* and *Marriage,* realistic as they are, are represented as being written some years hence, our own time already appearing retrospectively in them.   As little as Faust has he been tempted to call out upon the passing moment. His main characters drift through this period of time, substantial themselves but with a background of insubstantialities, in a way that recalls Paolo and Francesca looming out of the phantom cloud-procession of the *Inferno.*

Into this larger world, in short, he has carried with him only himself and his own story. We live in two worlds—the primary world of vivid personal realities and the secondary world of our human background.   It is the secondary world that anchors us in time and space; the primary world we carry with us as part of ourselves.   In Wells there is no secondary world, no human background, no sense of abiding relations.   It is his philosophy of life and the quality of his men and women to be experi-

mental in a plastic scheme. His range is very
small: the same figures reappear constantly.
There is the Wells hero,—Lewisham, Capes,
Ponderevo, Remington, Trafford, Stratton;
there is the Wells heroine, Ann Veronica, Isa-
bel, Marjorie, Lady Mary; there is the ineffectual woman with whom the Wells hero becomes entangled, Capes's first wife, Marion,
Margaret; there is the ineffectual man with
whom the Wells heroine becomes entangled,
Magnet, Manning. To strike the lowest common denominator in this tangle is inevitably to
arrive once more, one feels, in the region of
personal experience. Although it cannot be
said that his minor characters are lacking in
reality, they are certainly intellectual portraits,
and outside the limits of subjective experience.
The principal men and women of Wells move
through a world seen, but hardly a world felt.

This want of social background makes his
characters as detached from the familiar earth
as chessmen are detached from a chessboard.
They never seem to be, like most men and
women either in life or fiction, like the Kipps
and Polly of his own earlier fiction, vegetable

growths. Heredity, fatality, the soil are not mainly operating forces with them. They are creatures of intelligence and free will, freely and intelligently making and moulding themselves and their circumstances. Human nature in Wells is very largely a sheer thing, a thing that begins with itself, answers for itself, lives at first hand. That is the personal quality of the man himself, and it follows that the quality is wholly convincing only where what I have called his primary world is concerned: the rest of the world he builds up by intelligent observation and the literary talent of creating human stuff out of whole cloth.

In this he is well served by his antipathies. His belief in personal self-determinism is so strong that he instinctively sees the vegetative nature of the ordinary life as a kind of moral slough, a state of being detestably without initiative, faith, energy, will. And consequently the Normal Social Life against which he is always tilting is a life seen by him with all the vividness of an intense personal and philosophical animosity. Consider, for example, the portraits of Mr. Pope and Mr. Stanley, survivals

in a sense of the old Sir Roger de Coverley
type, with all the sweetness gone out of it and
only the odious qualities left, the domineering,
vain, proprietary qualities. They exist mainly
as symbols of everything that enlightened and
right-minded daughters will not put up with;
they come as near to being the foils of right
destiny as Wells will ever allow; they sum up
everything that stands in the way of man's
free will. They are mercilessly dealt with, and
they are memorable figures.

Without this antipathy, and outside his own
primary world, he pretty generally fails. One
recalls, for example, old Mrs. Trafford in *Marriage,* evidently intended to be his ideal of the
enlightened woman grown old. She is a pale,
dimly perfect, automatically wise old lady
carved out of wood. Trafford himself, one
feels, is a chip of the same block. Trafford
obviously is not Wells himself, as Ponderevo
and Remington are Wells: he is the Utopian
counterpart of these persons, at least in the
matter that concerns Wells most, the matter of
sex. One could show that, aside from the six
or eight chief characters who in their various

ways express the nature and experience of Wells himself, he succeeds in his portraiture only where no demand is made on his sympathies.

The same absence of social background which throws into relief his primary world of characters throws into relief also the primary facts of human nature. Trafford and Marjorie, the most conventionally placed of his characters, pull up stakes, leave their children, and go to Labrador. His other men and women are even more independent of the social network. Consequently they are independent of that chain of relationships—friendship, affection, minor obligations—which mitigate, subdue, soften the primary motives of most people. They are almost startlingly physical. Their instincts are as sure as those of cavemen, and their conduct as direct. They are as clear about the essential matter of love as ever Schopenhauer was, or Adam and Eve, and they stand out as sharply against the embarrassments and secrecies of the usual world as a volcanic rock stands out against a tropical landscape. In this without doubt they exhibit

the fact that socialism does and will actually
alter human nature, and that in the instinctive
socialist human nature is already altered. For
socialism inflexibly militates against those
more sentimental aspects of love, love of country as such, the paternal and feudal principles,
love of property, and the like, which belong
properly to the intelligence, all those functions
where love, in a majority of cases, goes wrong,
blunders, stultifies growth, confuses the public
design of the world. As a result it throws love
into relief, emphasizes the nature of sex and
the *raison d'être* of reproduction; makes it, to
use a favorite word of Wells, stark.

I pause at this word. It is one of those talis-
manic words one finds perpetually cropping up
in the writings of men who have a marked
point of view, words that express deep and
abiding preferences and often set the key of
an entire philosophy. "I like bare things,"
says George Ponderevo, in *Tono-Bungay;*
"stripped things, plain, austere, and continent
things, fine lines and cold colors." That is the
gesture of an artistic mind which repudiates,
with an impatient sharpness, all the entangle-

ments of the ordinary world. It is Oriental, it
is Japanese, it is anything you like; but if it is
English also it marks an entirely new regime.
Without question it is English, and American
as well. Thousands of people share that pref-
erence, and were economic socialism to go by
the board we should still have to reckon with
the progress of socialistic human nature. It
detaches itself each day a little more from
property, locality, and the hope of reward; it
ceases to be necessitarian, it becomes voluntary;
it relegates drudgery to mechanical devices; it
releases the individual to a sense of his own co-
operative and contributory place in the scheme
of a more orderly future. Relatively speaking, the tendency of our kind is all away from
luxury, sloth, complacency, confusion, ignorance, filth, heat, proprietorship, and all in the
direction of light, austerity, agility, intelligence, coolness, athletic energy, understanding, cleanliness, order, "bare things, fine lines,
and cold colors."

  That is evident, and it is equally evident that
the personal character and career of Wells are
emblematic of this entire tendency. He has

unravelled himself by science, talent, and vigor
out of "lower middle class" Victorianism. Is
it strange that he has adopted as a kind of
sacred image that light, free, and charming
product of our decade, the aeroplane, sprung
as it is out of the wreckage, out of the secret
beginnings, the confused muscularities, the effort and smoke of the most chaotic of all centuries, like a blade of exquisitely tempered and
chased steel which justifies everything that was
most laborious and unsightly in the forge?

But considered as a sacred image the aeroplane has its limitations. So also, considered
as an exponent of life, has Wells. Philosophy
and religion, as he presents them, are simply
what he chooses to think and feel, what he has
been led by his own experience to think and
feel. His main experience has been the experience of disentangling himself, and therefore
life, reflected from within himself, is to him a
thing also which disentangles itself and grows
ever more free, simple, and lucid. In the mind
of Wells this process has taken on an altogether mystical, transcendental significance, a
religious aspect. Possible as that is to himself

personally, how far can it be taken as an argument to the human soul? How does it qualify him as a teacher, a public voice, a thinker for the mass of men? How does the conception of life purely as a process relate itself to human experience?

Applied to history, it seems to fail. Wells is devoid of historical imagination. In his portrait of Margaret in *The New Machiavelli* he has properly, though somewhat harshly, repudiated what ordinarily passes for culture. But had he himself possessed the reality of what seems to him simply "living at second hand," he would never have been led to refer to Leonardo, Michael Angelo, and Dürer as "pathetically reaching out, as it were, with empty desirous hands toward the unborn possibilities of the engineer." That is a very interesting and a very extraordinary statement, and it is quite true that each of these men would have rejoiced in the engineering possibilities of our time. But how much of the soul of Michael Angelo, for example, was involved in engineering? How far can his hands be said to have been "empty" for the want of scope in

engineering? The power and the function of
Michael Angelo can rightly be seen, not in relation to any sort of social or mechanical process, but in relation to things that are permanent in human nature, in relation to just those
matters included in the admonition of Wells
to "reject all such ideas as Right, Liberty,
Happiness, Duty, and Beauty and hold fast to
the assertion of the fundamental nature of life
as a tissue and succession of births." Again,
consider a somewhat similar reference to Marcus Aurelius, of which the gist is that the au-
thor of the *Meditations* was, actually in consequence of his own character, the father of one
of the worst rulers the world has known. The
implication here is that the study of self-per-
fection in the father was complementary to, if
not responsible for, the social impotence and
blindness of the son. Instead of dedicating
himself to the static ideal of personal character, the assumption seems to be, Marcus
Aurelius ought to have lived exclusively in his
function as ruler and father. He studied himself, not as a ruler but as a man, and the social
process had its revenge on his line. To Wells,

in a word, the static elements of character and the study of perfection are not to be distinguished from vicious self-consequence.

Consider also a recent passage in which he has given a general impression of literature:

It seems to me more and more as I live longer that most poetry and most literature and particularly the literature of the past is discordant with the vastness and variety, the reserves and resources and recuperations of life as we live it to-day. It is the expression of life under cruder and more rigid conditions than ours, lived by people who loved and hated more naïvely, aged sooner, and died younger than we do. Solitary persons and single events dominated them as they do not dominate us.

To appreciate this meditation one has to remember the character and career which led to the writing of it. But so far as we others are concerned, how far can the assumption it rests upon be considered valid, the assumption of a process that sweeps men on and leads human nature, as it were, progressively to shed itself? Dr. Johnson, for example, was a man the conditions of whose life were crude and rigid in the extreme, a man singularly dominated by solitary persons and single events, but is his conversation discordant with the variety, the "reserves, resources, and recuperations of life as we live it to-day"? I can well understand this feeling. To pass directly from the thin, tentative, exhilarating, expansive air of our own time into the presence of that funny, stuffy, cocksure, pompous old man is to receive a preposterous shock. But having come to laugh, one stops with a very different sensation. The depths of personality and wisdom that exist there take on a disconcerting significance in relation to contemporary pragmatism. The mass of men veer about; far-separated epochs have their elective affinities, and if anything about the future is plain it is that this, that, and the other generation will find in Dr. Johnson a strangely premature contemporary.

Wells has himself admitted this principle. To Plutarch, Rabelais, Machiavelli he has paid his tribute. Hear what George Ponderevo has to say about Plutarch in his recollections of Bladesover House:

I found Langhorne's *Plutarch* too, I remember, on those shelves. It seems queer to me now to think that

I acquired pride and self-respect, the idea of a state and the germ of public spirit, in such a furtive fashion; queer, too, that it should rest with an old Greek, dead these eighteen hundred years, to teach me that.

Considering what part the notion of a state plays in his range of ideas, that is a remarkable confession. But why stop with statecraft? The human mind could not, in all epochs, have established permanent ideals of statecraft without permanent ideals of a more strictly personal kind.

The truth is that Wells, for all that he has passed outside the economics of socialism, is really bounded by the circle of ideas which produced them. The typical Marxian, the concentrated Marxian, will tell you that life is summed up in the theory of value, and that the only true thing is economic determinism. Measuring all thought by that criterion, he finds Dante and Shakespeare unintelligible and offensive gibberish, and will scent the trail of the capitalist in Grimm's Fairy Tales. That is the crude form in which exclusive socialism presents itself. To say that "the fundamental nature of life is a tissue and succession of births" is merely a refinement of this.   It is true, just as the economic determinism of Marx on the whole is true.   But the world is full of a number of things; or rather it is the business of a reasonable mind to see it in a number of ways at once.   Because there is a Will to Live and a Will to Power, because things grow and continue to grow, that does not explain love, or pain, or friendship, or music, or poetry, or indeed life.   Life is a tangle, a tangle which every socialist must feel to be disentangling itself; but it is also a riddle, and on that point socialism has nothing to say at all.

It is in presenting life wholly as a tangle and not at all as a riddle that the philosophy and religion of Wells appear so inadequate. Could Wells write a poem? one asks oneself, and the question is full of meaning.   There is nothing to suggest that at any moment of his life he has felt this impulse, which has been the normal thing in English authors.   "Modern poetry, with an exception or so," he remarks somewhere, and for all his writings reveal of him he might have said poetry as a whole, "does not signify at all."   It is the same with regard

to music, art, external nature. He is not wanting in the plastic sense: his writings are filled
with picturesque groupings, figures cut in out-
line against a sunset, masses of machinery in
the glare of the forge, things that suggest the
etcher's eye. But they are curiously impersonal. Consider, for example, his description
of Worms Cathedral:

> It rises over this green and flowery peace, a towering,
> lithe, light brown, sunlit, easy thing, as unconsciously
> and irrelevantly splendid as a tall ship in the evening
> glow under a press of canvas.

You cannot doubt that he has felt a beauty
in this, but the beauty he feels is essentially
the beauty of a piece of engineering; he is as
untouched by the strictly personal artistic and
religious qualities of this building, not to men-
tion its connection with human history, as if he
had seen it through a telescope from another
planet. It is not the changeless riddle and par-
tial solution of life for which this building
stands that stir in Wells the sense of beauty
and meaning: it is the mechanism, the process
—his emotions gather about the physical result
which appears to justify these.

À chacun son infini.

There will always be some to whom the significance of things, the meaning of any given present will seem to evaporate in this conception of mankind as "permanently in transition." Reading those passages where Wells has expressed the meaning life has for him, I feel much as I should feel with regard to music if I heard a mass of Mozart played at the rate of sixty beats a second, or, with regard to painting, if a procession of Rembrandts were moved rapidly across my field of vision. The music as a whole is a tissue and succession of sounds, the pictures as a whole are a tissue and succession of colors. But that is not music, that is not art. Nor is a tissue and succession of births life.

But indeed nothing is easier than to reduce Wells to an absurdity. If he implies anything at all he implies a "transvaluation of all values." It remains to consider him from this point of view.

Chapter VII

THE SPIRIT OF WELLS

IN order to understand Wells at all one must grasp the fact that he belongs to a type of mind which has long existed in European literature but which is comparatively new in the English-speaking world, the type of mind of the so-called "intellectual." He is an "intellectual" rather than an artist; that is to say, he naturally grasps and interprets life in the light of ideas rather than in the light of experience.

To pass from a definition to an example, let me compare Wells in this respect with the greatest and most typical figure of the opposite camp in contemporary English fiction; I mean Joseph Conrad. This comparison is all the more apt because just as much as Wells Conrad typifies the spirit of "unrest" (a word he has almost made his own, so often does he use it) which is the note of our age. Both of these

novelists have endeavored to express the spirit
of unrest; both have suggested a way of making it contributory to the attainment of an
ideal. But how different is their method, how
different is their ideal! And roughly the difference is this: that to Conrad the spirit of
unrest is a personal mood, a thing, as people
used to say, between man and his Maker;
whereas to Wells the spirit of unrest is not a
mood but a rationally explicable frame of
mind, a sense of restricted function, an issue to
be fought out not between man and nature but
between man and society. In other words,
where Conrad's point of view is moral, Wells's
point of view is social; and whereas in Conrad
the spirit of unrest can only be appeased by
holding fast to certain simple instinctive moral
principles, integrity, honor, loyalty, etc., contributing in this way to the ideal of personal
character, the spirit of unrest in Wells is to be
appeased by working through the established
fact, by altering the environment in which man
lives, contributing in this way to the ideal of a
great society of which personal character is at
once the essence and the product.

In the end, of course, both these views of life come to the same thing, for you cannot have a great society which is not composed of greatly living individuals, or vice versa. But practically there is a world of difference between them, according as any given mind emphasizes the one or the other. This difference, I say, is the difference between life approached through experience and life approached through ideas. And when we penetrate behind these points of view we find that they are determined very largely by the characters and modes of living of the men who hold them. That explains the vital importance in literary criticism of knowing something about the man one is discussing, as distinguished from the work of his brain pure and simple. There is a reason why the intellectualist point of view occurs as a rule in men who have habitually lived the delocalized, detached, and comparatively depersonalized life of cities, while men of the soil, of the sea, of the elements, men, so to speak, of intensive experience, novelists like Conrad or Tolstoy or Hardy, are fundamentally non-intellectual, pessimistic, and moral.

And this explains the natural opposition between Conrad and Wells. Aside from the
original bent of his mind, the intensive quality
of Conrad's experience—an experience of ships
and the minute, simple, personal, tragic life of
ships, set off against the impersonal, appalling
sea and an always indifferent universe, a life
remote from change, in which the relations of
things are in a peculiar sense abiding and in
which only one problem exists, the problem of
character, imminent nature being kept at bay
only through the loyalty, integrity and grit of
men—the intensive quality of this experience,
I say, acting upon an artistic mind, would naturally tend to produce not only a bitterly profound wisdom, but an equally profound contempt for the play of ideas, so irresponsible in
comparison, and for a view of the world based
upon ideas the real cost of which has never
been counted in the face of hunger, icy winds,
storm and shipwreck, and the abysmal forces
of nature. Men who go down to the sea in
ships have a right to say for themselves (tempering the credulity of those who have remained at home) that the intellectualist view

of life is altogether too easy and too glib. It is they who throw into relief the deep, obscure conviction of the "plain man"—commonly the good man—that to endeavor to make life conform with ideas is in some way to deprive the world of just those elements which create character and to strike at an ideal forged through immemorial suffering and effort.

Merely to dismiss as dumb folly an all but universal contention of this kind (no doubt in the back of people's minds when they say that socialism, for instance, is "against human nature") is to beg the whole question of intellectualism itself. For, if it could be conclusively shown that any view of life not incidentally but by its nature emasculated life and destroyed the roots of character, then of course, no matter how rationally self-evident it might be and how much confusion and suffering it might avert, it would never even justify its own reason for being—it would never *succeed,* the best part of human nature would oppose it to the end of time and the intelligence itself would be discredited. And indeed to the man of experience rather than the

man of ideas, just because of his rich humanity, just because he never passes out of the
personal range, belong the ideal things, morality, philosophy, art. Like charity, these
things "begin at home"; and whenever (as in
pragmatism, when pragmatism ceases to be a
method and claims to be an interpretation of
life) they are approached not from the side of
experience but from the side of ideas they
cease to have any real substance. ° Morality has
no substance when it springs from the mind instead of the conscience, art when it appeals to
the mind instead of the perceptions; and as to
philosophy, what is any scheme of things that
springs out of the head of a man who is not
himself wise? It is a certain condemnation of
Bergson, for example, that he would never pass
muster in a group of old fishermen smoking
their pipes on the end of a pier. ·Not that they
would be expected in any case to know what
he was talking about, but that his fibre so
plainly is the fibre not of a wise but of a clever
man and that in everything, as Emerson said,
you must have a source higher than your tap.

That is why, as it seems to me, Wells ought

not to be considered from any of these absolute standpoints.   He has put before us not so much a well-wrought body of artistic work, or a moral programme, or an explanation of life —words quite out of place in connection with him—as a certain new spirit, filled with all sorts of puzzled intimations of a new beauty and even a new religion to be generated out of a new order of things that is only glimpsed at present.   And the point I should like to make about this spirit is that it is entirely irrelevant to the values of life as we know them, but that it may in the end prove to have contributed to an altogether fresh basis for human values.

To illustrate what I mean by this irrelevance as regards present values and this possibility as regards future values let me turn to that long brilliant passage in *The New Machiavelli* where Remington goes from club to club, passing in review the spiritual possibilities of each political party, and finds nothing but a desolation of triviality, pomposity, confusion, and "utterly damned old men."   Consider the contempt and hopelessness that fill his mind.   One has to forget entirely the ordinary man's view

of politics, sincerely held as it is; one has to
think of politics as a means of straightening
out and re-engendering a whole world of confused anguish before one can see any justifi-
cation for this righteous wit and savage indig-
nation against the dulness of leaders.   Considered by the current values of life in which
politics are regarded as an effect of man's incompetence rather than as a cause of his virtue,
treated intensively, as a novelist of experience
rather than of ideas would have treated them,
in what a different light each of these "utterly
damned old men" would appear, each one a
tiny epic of tragic and comic efforts, disap-
pointments, misconceptions, providing one in
the end with how much of an excuse for blame,
ridicule or contempt!   Everything indeed depends upon where a given mind chooses to lay
emphasis.   In this scene Wells has judged
everything by his ideal of a great society, just
as Conrad, faced with the same material,
would have judged everything by his ideal of
personal character.   Conrad would have used
those men to give us an understanding of life
as it is, whereas Wells has used them simply to

throw into relief his idea of what life ought to be. Conrad would have created a work of art, illustrated a moral programme, and interpreted life. Wells, admittedly a clever caricaturist, only rises above the level of a clever caricaturist according as we accept the validity of his ideal and share the spirit in which he writes. Like many children of light, Wells is not wise in his own generation. But perhaps another generation will justify him.

If Wells had lingered in these deep realities of his own time he would have been a greater artist. And indeed so marked has been his own development away from the world of ideas and toward the world of experience that were he to begin afresh it is likely that he would resemble the type of novelist of which I have taken Conrad as an example far more than his former self. Of socialism he has abandoned all the theories and most of the schemes and retained only the frame of mind. He has taken year by year a more intensive view of life, he has grown too conscious of the inertia that impedes ideas and the overwhelming immediacies of the actual world to be called glib and easy any more. "How little and feeble is the life of man, a thing of chances, preposterously unable to find the will to realize even the most timid of its dreams!" he says in one of his latest novels, and if he has kept alive his faith in ideas, who will deny that he has begun to count the cost of it?

From this side, I think, it is no longer possible for anyone to assail him, so frankly has he given hostages to "actuality." It is from the other side, his own side, and especially in the light of his own ideal, that an answer is required for the slackness which has come upon him and which is very marked in his recent novels. Is it possible to ignore the fact that since he wrote *The New Machiavelli* the work of Wells has lived on its capital and lost the passionate curiosity and personal conviction that made him the force he was in our epoch? Always unwilling to check his talent and publish only the results of his genuine mental progress, he has become, in spite of splendid moments, too much of the common professional novelist, dealing with levels and phases of life where he obviously does not belong, astray from his own natural point of intense contact with things. I want to avoid the usual habit of critics who think it their business to put authors in their places, but is it not a fact that Wells understands the Kippses and Pollys far better than the lords and ladies of England and that he was at his best in elaborating a bridge—a wonderful visionary bridge—between the little world of dumb routine and the great world of spacious initiatives? Carlyle with his Great Man theory, forged out of his own travail and weakness, in the end fell on his knees before the illusion of lordship. Fifteen years ago one might have predicted the same future for the Samurai of Wells, not because the Samurai are themselves equivocal but because Wells is an Englishman. There so plainly to the English mind the great gentlemen are, the men who can and the men who never do! Towards this Circe of the English imagination Wells has travelled with a fatal consistency, and the result to be foreseen was first of all fatuity and in the end extinction.

After he had written *The New Machiavelli*

Wells had reached a point where his ideas, in
order to be saved, had to be rescued from himself. To believe that life can be straightened
out by the intelligence is necessarily to have
"travelled light," in a measure; too much experience is the end of that frame of mind. In
Tono-Bungay and *The New Machiavelli* ideas
and experience met in a certain invisible point
—that is the marvel which has made these books
unique and, I suppose, permanent; the greatest possible faith in ideas was united with the
greatest possible grasp of everything that impedes them. One had therefore a sense of
tragic struggle, in which the whole life of our
time was caught up and fiercely wrestled with;
one had the feeling that here was the greatest
moment in the life of a writer suddenly become
great. But with these books some secret virtue
seems to have passed out of Wells. Since then
his ideas have been hardly more than a perfunctory repetition and his experience more
and more remote and unreal; and looking back
one seems to discover something highly sym-
bolic in the tragical conquest of ideas by pas-

sion with which *The New Machiavelli* con-
cludes.

But indeed Wells was always a man whose
ideas were greater than himself. "I stumble
and flounder," says George Ponderevo, "but I
know that over all these merry immediate
things, there are other things that are great
and serene, very high, beautiful things—the
reality. I haven't got it, but it's there nevertheless. I'm a spiritual guttersnipe in love
with unimaginable goddesses." And just for
this reason the spirit which in his great days
possessed him is independent of any fate that
may befall Wells himself and his art. More
than this, by frankly and fully testing his ideas
in a life-and-death struggle with reality he has,
even at the cost of his own shipwreck, removed
from the cause of ideas the greatest reproach
which has always been brought against it.
Revolutionists, doctrinaires, idealogues have
notoriously failed to test the validity of their
ideas even in the face of their own private passions and confusions; they have rarely considered for a moment that their own lives totally
unfit them for supposing that men are natu-

rally good and that to make reason prevail is one of the simplest operations in the world. Wells, on the other hand, has consistently shown that theory divorced from practice is a mode of charlatanism, that "love and fine thinking" must go together, and that precisely because of man's individual incapacity to live, as things are, with equal honesty the life of ideas and the life of experience, the cause he has at heart must be taken out of the hands of the individual and made to form a common impersonal will and purpose in the mind of the race as a whole.

Intellectualism, in fact, the view that life can be determined by ideas (and of this socialism is the essence) if it can be justified at all has to be justified in the face of all current human values. It is based on an assumption, a grand and generous assumption, I maintain, and one that has to take what is called a sporting chance with all the odds against it.   This assumption is, that on the whole human nature can be trusted to take care of itself while the surplus energy of life, com-

monly absorbed in the struggle against incapacity, sloth, perversity, and disorder ("original sin," to sum it all up), is released for the
organization of a better scheme for mankind; and further, that this better scheme,
acting on a race naturally capable of a richer and fuller life, will have the effect on
men as a whole that re-environing has on any
cramped, ill-nourished, unventilated organism,
and that art, religion, morals (all that makes
up the substance and meaning of life) instead
of being checked and blighted in the process
will in the end, strong enough to bear trans-
plantation, be re-engendered on a finer and
freer basis. This, in a word, is the contention
of the intellectual, a splendid gambler's chance,
on which the future rests, and to which people
have committed themselves more than they
know. It is a bridge thrown out across the
void, resting at one end on the good intentions
of mankind and relying at the other upon mankind's fulfilling those good intentions. It is
based like every great enterprise of the modern
world upon credit, and its only security is the
fact that men thus far and on the whole have

measured up to each enlargement of their freedom and responsibility.

To feel the force of this one has to think of the world as a world. Just here has been the office of socialism, to show that society is a colossal machine of which we are all parts and that men in the most exact sense are members one of another. In the intellectualist scheme of things that mathematical proof has to come first; it has to take root and bury itself and become the second nature of humankind before the new world of instinct can spring out of it and come to blossom.

That has been the office of socialism, and just so far as that proof has been established socialism has played its part. Now the point I want to make about Wells is that in him one sees already in an almost precocious form the second stage of this process. In him this new world of intelligence is already exuberant with instinct; the social machine has become a personality; that cold abstraction the world has become in his hands a throbbing, breathing, living thing, as alive, awake, aware of itself, as engaging, adventurous, free, critical, well-primed, continent, and all-of-a-piece as a strong man running a race. People never felt nature as a personality before Wordsworth showed them that it was, or a locomotive before Kipling wrote *McAndrew's Hymn;* and it seems to me that Wells has done for the social organism very much what Wordsworth did for nature, discovering in a thing previously felt to be inanimate a matter for art and a basis for religious emotion.

But if the world is a personality it is a very stupid, sluggish, unawakened personality, differing from nature in this respect, that we ourselves compose the whole of it and have it in our hands to do what we will with it. It has always been out of joint, a great slipshod Leviathan, at sixes and sevens, invertebrate and fungus-brained. Just so is the average man, sunk in routine, oppressed with microscopic tasks that give birth one to another, his stomach at war with his head, his legs unwilling to exercise him, resentful of his own capacity not to be dull. But certain happier moments bring him an exuberant quickened life in which routine tasks fall nimbly from his fingers and he is

aware of a wide, humorous, generous, enlightened vision of things; he pulls himself together,
his parts reinforce one another, his mind
wakens, his heart opens, his fancy stirs, he is
all generosity and happiness, capable of anything that is disinterested, fine, and becoming
to a free man. It is in these moments that individual men have done all the things which
make up the real history of this planet.

If individual men are capable of this amazing experience, then why not the world? That
is the spirited question Wells has propounded
in a hundred different forms, in his earlier,
more theoretical, and more optimistic writings
suggesting that society as a whole should turn
over a new leaf, and even picturing it as doing
so, in his later work, more experienced and less
hopeful but with a compensating fervor, picturing the attempt of delegated individuals to
act on society's behalf. I do not wish at this
point to become pious and solemn in tone; that
would be inept in connection with Wells. But
I do wish to make it plain that if he is devoid
of those grander traits which spring from the
sense of being "tenon'd and mortised" upon

something beyond change, if his strength lies
wholly in his intelligence, the intelligence itself
in Wells is an amazing organ, a troubled and
rapturous organ, an organ as visionary and
sensitive as the soul of a Christian saint. That
is why I have said that in him the new world,
governed by the intelligence, is already exuberant with instinct; and anyone who doubts that
he has lavished a very genuine religious instinct
upon the social process itself and in the dream
of a society free, magnanimous and seemly,
should turn to the passage where he describes
Machiavelli, after the heat and pettiness of the
day, retiring into his chamber alone, putting
on his dress of ceremony and sitting down before his table in the presence of that magnificent thought.

The mass of men have acted more consistently than they know on the principle that the
whole world is nothing in comparison with one
soul, for their politics and economic science,
solemn as they appear, are as frivolous and
secondary as if they actually did believe fer-
vently that heaven is their true home and the
world a bad business of little account. In all

that concerns private virtue and the private
life, in religion, poetry, their lawyer, their doctor, their broker, they exact the last degree of
excellence and efficiency, but they trust to the
blind enterprise of individual men to push mankind chaotically forward little by little.   We
are in fact so wonderfully made that if our
grocer tells us in the morning that he has no
fresh eggs he throws us into a deeper despon-
dency than six readings of the *Inferno* could
ever do.   And that explains why so few people
can extend themselves imaginatively into the
greater circles that surround them, why, on the
social plane, we never think of demanding wisdom from politicians, why we never dream of
remembering that they should belong to the
august family of Plutarch, why it is not the
profound views of wise men and the brilliant
discoveries of science that fill the newspapers,
but the incredibly banal remarks of this presi-
dent and that prime minister, why presidents
and prime ministers in a society that lives from
hand to mouth are so much more important
than poets and prophets, and why statesmanship has gathered about itself a literature so

incomparably trivial and dull. Socialists, indeed, just because they alone are serious about the world, are apt to be the least mundane in spirit; they are, as Wells has himself said, "other-worldly" about the world itself.

But indeed I should make a mistake were I to over-stress the solemnities that underlie the spirit of Wells. In tone he is more profane than sacred, that is to say he is a realist. He wants a world thrillingly alive, curious, exercised, magnanimous, with all its dim corners lighted up, shaken out of its dulness and complacency, keen, elastic, tempered like a fine blade—the counterpart on a grand scale of what he most admires in the individual. "Stephen," says Lady Mary in *The Passionate Friends,* "promise me. Whatever you become, you promise and swear here and now never to be grey and grubby, never to be humpy and snuffy, never to be respectable and modest and dull and a little fat, like—like everybody." And in *First and Last Things* he gives the other side of the medal:

Much more to me than the desire to live is the desire to taste life. I am not happy until I have done and felt things. I want to get as near as I can to the thrill of a dog going into a fight or the delight of a bird in the air. And not simply in the heroic field of war and the air do I want to understand. I want to know something of the jolly wholesome satisfaction that a hungry pig must find in its wash. I want to get the fine quintessence of that.

It stands to reason that a spirit of this kind does not consort with any pre-arranged pocket ground-plan, so to speak, of the world as it should be. Of this, to be sure, he is often accused, and he has given us a humorous version of his Utopia as it may appear to certain of his contemporaries:

Mr. G. K. Chesterton mocks valiantly and passionately, I know, against an oppressive and obstinately recurrent anticipation of himself in Socialist hands, hair clipped, meals of a strictly hygienic description at regular hours, a fine for laughing, not that he would want to laugh, and austere exercises in several of the more metallic virtues daily. Mr. Max Beerbohm's conception is rather in the nature of a nightmare, a hopeless, horrid, frozen flight from the pursuit of Mr. Sidney Webb and myself, both of us short, inelegant men, but for all that terribly resolute, indefatigable, incessant to capture him, to drag him off to a mechanical Utopia, and then to take his thumb-mark and his name, number him distinctly in indelible ink, and let him loose (under inspection) in a

world of great round lakes of blue lime-water and vistas
of white sanitary tiling.

That is a not unjust parody of Wells's Utopia as it would be if he had remained in the
circle of his Fabian friends. Being what he
is, it bears much the same relation to his idea
as that world of harps and crowns and milk
and honey bore in the mediæval imagination
to the idea of heaven. You have to mingle
these notions with your experience of human
hearts to realize the inadequacy of symbols.
Wells, I suspect, has a fondness for white sanitary tiling, just as plenty of good Christians
have found in milk and honey a foretaste of
unthinkable felicity; but when it comes to the
actual architecture and domestic arrangements
of paradise they are both quite willing to take
on trust the accommodating good will of God
and man. Somehow or other, by the time we
have got there, we shall not find it monotonous
—to this, at least, one's faith, whatever it may
be, ought to be equal.

I have given too few quotations in this book,
and now I have left it to a point where if I
give any at all it must be to illustrate less the

art of Wells as a thing by itself than a train of
thought. He is at his best in brief scenes,
where all his gifts of humor, satire, characteri-
zation and phrase come to a head (think, for
example, of Aunt Plessington's speech, the
funeral of Mr. Polly's father, the pages dealing with Cousin Nicodemus Frapp's house-
hold, and the somewhat prolonged episode of
the "reet Staffordshire" cousins in *The New
Machiavelli*) ; and indeed, so insistent is his
point of view that in every one of these episodes one finds in opposition the irrepressible
new world of Wells and the stagnant world
out of which it springs. One of the best of
these scenes, luckily, is brief and connected
enough to be quoted as a whole. It is a picture
of the tea-hour in the servants' hall at Bladesover House.

I sat among these people on a high, hard, early Gre-
gorian chair, trying to exist, like a feeble seedling amidst
great rocks, and my mother sat with an eye upon me,
resolute to suppress the slightest manifestation of vi-
tality. It was hard on me, but perhaps it was also hard
upon these rather over-fed, ageing, pretending people,
that my youthful restlessness and rebellious unbelieving
eyes should be thrust in among their dignities.

Tea lasted for nearly three-quarters of an hour, and I sat it out perforce; and day after day the talk was exactly the same.

"Sugar, Mrs. Mackridge?" my mother used to ask. "Sugar, Mrs. Latude-Fernay?"

The word sugar would stir the mind of Mrs. Mackridge. "They say," she would begin, issuing her proclamation—at least half her sentences began "they say"—"sugar is fatt-an-ing, nowadays. Many of the best people do not take it at all."

"Not with their tea, ma'am," said Rabbits, intelligently.

"Not with anything," said Mrs. Mackridge, with an air of crushing repartee, and drank.

"What won't they say next?" said Miss Fison.

"They do say such things!" said Mrs. Booch.

"They say," said Mrs. Mackridge, inflexibly, "the doctors are not recomm-an-ding it now."

My Mother: "No, ma'am?"

Mrs. Mackridge: "No, ma'am."

Then, to the table at large: "Poor Sir Roderick, before he died, consumed great quan-ta-ties of sugar. I have sometimes fancied it may have hastened his end."

This ended the first skirmish. A certain gloom of manner and a pause was considered due to the sacred memory of Sir Roderick.

"George," said my mother, "don't kick the chair!"

Then, perhaps, Mrs. Booch would produce a favorite piece from her repertoire. "The evenings are drawing out nicely," she would say, or if the season was decadent, "How the evenings draw in!" It was an invaluable remark to her; I do not know how she would have got along without it.

My mother, who sat with her back to the window, would always consider it due to Mrs. Booch to turn about and regard the evening in the act of elongation or contraction, whichever phase it might be.

A brisk discussion of how long we were to the longest or shortest day would ensue, and die away at last exhausted.

There is, I think, a special sort of connection between Wells and America; and there are times when it seems to me that were the spirit of America suddenly to become critical of itself it would resemble nothing in the world so much as the spirit of Wells magnified by many diameters. His instincts are all as it were instincts of the intelligence; his mind, like the American mind, is a disinherited mind, not connected with tradition, thinking and acting *de novo* because there is nothing to prevent it from doing so. Perfectly American is his alertness, his versatility, adaptability, his thorough-going pragmatism, perfectly American are the disconcerting questions that he asks ("Is the Navy *bright?*"). Perfectly Ameri-

can is his view of the traditional English ideal
of human nature—that strange compound
of good intentions, homely affection, stubborn
strength, insensibility to ideas, irrational self-
sacrifice, domestic despotism, a strong sense of
property in things and people, stupidity,
sweetness and confusion of mind—an ideal
through which it has been one of his never-
failing delights to send electric shocks. And
indeed the type of character he has presented
in his heroes, in Remington, Trafford and Ponderevo, is a type to be found perhaps more
plentifully than elsewhere in American research bureaus, hospitals and laboratories. He
thinks and feels critically so many of the
things America lives and does unconsciously.
Perhaps in this distinction lies the immediate
value of his criticism for us.

For in his mind Americans can see themselves reflected in the light of what they chiefly
need, that synthetic motive without which a
secular and industrial race is as devoid of animating morality as a swarm of flies. This
want, most obvious on the political and economic plane, is indeed fundamental. Wells

has grasped it from many different angles but never with more point than in his essay *The American Population*. Consider this passage, where he takes as a text one of Arthur Brisbane's editorials in the "New York Journal":

It is the voice of the American tradition strained to the utmost to make itself audible to the new world, and cracking into italics and breaking into capitals with the strain. The rest of that enormous bale of paper is eloquent of a public void of moral ambitions, lost to any sense of comprehensive things, deaf to ideas, impervious to generalizations, a public which has carried the conception of freedom to its logical extreme of entire individual detachment. These telltale columns deal all with personality and the drama of personal life. They witness to no interest but the interest in intense individual experiences. The engagements, the love affairs, the scandals of conspicuous people are given in pitiless detail in articles adorned with vigorous portraits and sensational pictorial comments. Even the eavesdroppers who write this stuff strike the personal note, and their heavily muscular portraits frown beside the initial letter. Murders and crimes are worked up to the keenest pitch of realization, and any new indelicacy in fashionable costume, any new medical device or cure, any new dance or athleticism, any new breach in the moral code, any novelty in sea-bathing or the woman's seat on horseback, or the like, is given copious and moving illustration, stirring headlines, and eloquent reprobation. There is a colored supplement of knock-about fun, written chiefly in the quaint dialect of the New York slums. It is a language from which "th" has vanished, and it presents a world in which the kicking by a mule of an endless succession of victims is an inexhaustible joy to young and old. "Dat ole Maud!" There is a smaller bale dealing with sport. In the advertisement columns one finds nothing of books, nothing of art; but great choice of bust developers, hair restorers, nervous tonics, clothing sales, self-contained flats, and business opportunities. . . .

Individuality has, in fact, got home to itself, and, as people say, taken off its frills. . . . The "New York American" represents a clientèle to be counted by the hundred thousand, manifestly with no other solicitudes, just burning to live and living to burn.

Now that is a very fair picture, not merely of popular America but of the whole contemporary phase of popular civilization, uprooted from the state of instinct, intensive experience and the immemorial immediacies of duty and the soil. To the artist and the moralist it is a cause of hopeless pessimism, as any civilization must be which has lost touch with all its values and been rationalized to the point of anarchy. For this there is only one salvation. If civilization has lost the faculty of commanding it-

self and pulling itself together in its individual
aspect, it must pull itself together collectively.
That essentially is the fighting chance of intellectualism, the hope that, inasmuch as the
world has already lost touch with experience
and committed itself to a regime of ideas, by
organizing this regime of ideas and by mechan-
izing so far as possible the material aspect of
things, the values of life can be re-engendered
on a fresh basis.   From this follows the oft-
repeated phrase of Wells that the chief want
of the American people is a "sense of the
state." For the peril and the hope of American life (granting that, as things are, society
must be brought into some kind of coherence
before morality, art and religion can once more
attain any real meaning) lies in the fact that
while at present Americans are aware of themselves only as isolated individuals they are unconsciously engaged in works of an almost appalling significance for the future of society.
A Trust is a work of this kind, and whether
it is to be a gigantic good or a gigantic evil depends wholly upon whether its controlling
minds are more conscious of their individual or

their social function. The mechanism of society in America is already developed to a very high point; what is wanting, and without this everything is wanting, is an understanding of the right function of this mechanism. So much does it all depend upon whether the financial mind can subdue itself to the greater mind of the race.

If the future is anywhere going to follow the lines that Wells has suggested for it—and being an opportunist his aims are always in touch with agreeable probabilities—it will most likely be in America. He has lately given his idea of what the State should aim to be—"planned as an electric traction system is planned, without reference to pre-existing apparatus, upon scientific lines"; an idea remarkably of a piece with the American imagination and one which the American imagination is perfectly capable of translating into fact. American, too, are the methods in which Wells has come to believe for bringing the Great State into existence. His conviction is that socialism will come through an enlightened individualism, outside the recognized governmental institutions, and that the ostensible States will be superseded virtually by informal centres of gravity quite independent of them. America alone at present justifies this speculation. For the centre of gravity in American affairs has always been extra-governmental, and consistently in America where wealth gathers there also the institutions of socialism spring into being. The rudiments of the Socialist State, falsely based as they are but always tending to subvert this false basis, are certainly to be found, if anywhere, in the Rockefeller Institute, the Carnegie and Russell Sage Foundations, the endowed universities and bureaus of research, and in the type of men they breed. Consider the following passage from *The Passionate Friends* and the character of the American, Gidding, which is indicated in it:

To Gidding it was neither preposterous nor insufferably magnificent that we should set about a propaganda of all science, all knowledge, all philosophical and political ideas, round about the habitable globe. His mind began producing concrete projects as a firework being lit produces sparks, and soon he was "figuring out" the most colossal of printing and publishing projects, as a man might work out the particulars for an alteration to his bathroom. It was so entirely natural to him, it was so entirely novel to me, to go on from the proposition that understanding was the primary need of humanity to the systematic organization of free publishing, exhaustive discussion, intellectual stimulation. He set about it as a company of pharmacists might organize the distribution of some beneficial cure.

"Say, Stratton," he said, after a conversation that had seemed to me half fantasy, "let's *do* it."

It is perfectly possible in fact that socialism will come into being first of all under the form of Cecil Rhodes's dream, as a secret order of millionaires "promoting" not their own aims but society itself. That is one of the possibilities at least that lie in what Wells has called the "gigantic childishness" of the American mind.

INDEX

187